Petrarch'S Letters to Classical Authors

Mario Emilio Cosenza, Francesco Petrarca

Nabu Public Domain Reprints:

You are holding a reproduction of an original work published before 1923 that is in the public domain in the United States of America, and possibly other countries. You may freely copy and distribute this work as no entity (individual or corporate) has a copyright on the body of the work. This book may contain prior copyright references, and library stamps (as most of these works were scanned from library copies). These have been scanned and retained as part of the historical artifact.

This book may have occasional imperfections such as missing or blurred pages, poor pictures, errant marks, etc. that were either part of the original artifact, or were introduced by the scanning process. We believe this work is culturally important, and despite the imperfections, have elected to bring it back into print as part of our continuing commitment to the preservation of printed works worldwide. We appreciate your understanding of the imperfections in the preservation process, and hope you enjoy this valuable book.

PETRARCH'S LETTERS TO CLASSICAL AUTHORS

TRANSLATED FROM THE LATIN
WITH A COMMENTARY

BY

MARIO EMILIO COSENZA, Ph.D.
*Instructor in Latin in The College of the
City of New York*

CHICAGO
THE UNIVERSITY OF CHICAGO PRESS
1910

Ital 7138.19

HL Pierce

Copyright 1910 By
The University of Chicago

Published March 1910

Composed and Printed By
The University of Chicago Press
Chicago, Illinois, U. S. A.

TO MY MOTHER
AND
TO MY FATHER

TO MY MOTHER
AND
TO MY FATHER

CONTENTS

	PAGE
INTRODUCTION	ix
I. LETTER TO M. T. CICERO	1
Notes to Letter I	5
II. LETTER TO M. T. CICERO	21
Notes to Letter II	29
III. LETTER TO ANNAEUS SENECA	43
Notes to Letter III	55
IV. LETTER TO MARCUS VARRO	69
Notes to Letter IV	76
V. LETTER TO QUINTILIAN	84
Notes to Letter V	90
VI. LETTER TO TITUS LIVY	100
Notes to Letter VI	104
VII. LETTER TO ASINIUS POLLIO	112
Notes to Letter VII	118
VIII. LETTER TO HORATIUS FLACCUS	125
Notes to Letter VIII	132
IX. LETTER TO PUBLIUS VERGILIUS MARO	136
Notes to Letter IX	141
X. LETTER TO HOMER	148
Notes to Letter X	172
A SELECTED BIBLIOGRAPHY	205

INTRODUCTION

It is hardly necessary to dwell upon Petrarch's extensive correspondence. He was the leader of the learned men of his age; and it is common knowledge that all his prominent contemporaries—whether in the political world, or in the religious world, or in the scholarly world—were numbered among his friends.

Corresponding so incessantly with all men and on all topics, Petrarch's letters soon grew into an unmanageable mass. One day in 1359 (Frac., Note to *Fam.*, XXIV, 13) Petrarch, with a sigh, consigned to the flames a thousand or more papers, consisting of short poems and of letters, merely to avoid the irksome task of sifting and of correcting them. He then noticed a few papers lying in a corner, which (after some hesitation) he spared because they had already been recopied and arranged by his secretary (*Praefatio ad Socratem*, I, p. 15). Petrarch divided these "few" letters into two groups, dedicating the twenty-four books of prose epistles to Socrates (*Praefatio, loc. cit.*, and *Fam.*, XXIV, 13), and the three books of poetic epistles to Marco Barbato (*Praefatio, loc. cit.*, pp. 15, 16, and *Fam.*, XXII, 3).

Farther on in his prefatory letter to Socrates, Petrarch points out the vigor and the courage to be seen in his earlier letters, and advances extenuating circumstances for the laments which begin to crop out in the later ones. He excuses these by arguing that they were occasioned by the misfortunes which befell his friends, and not by those which he had suffered in his own person. At this point Petrarch does not lose the opportunity for comparing himself with Cicero. The passage gives so completely the information needed by the reader that it is hereby translated in full (*Praefatio*, I, p. 25):

Cicero, however, exhibits such weakness in his adversity that, although I am delighted with his style, I am oftentimes equally offended by his actions. Add to this his quarrelsome letters—the altercations and the reproachful language which he employs against the most illustrious men whom he has but recently been praising. It all reveals a remarkable fickleness of disposition. On reading these letters, I was soothed and ruffled at the same time. I could not restrain myself, and, indignation prompting me, I wrote to him as to a friend of my own years and time, regardless of the ages which separated us. Indeed, I wrote with a familiarity acquired through an intimate knowledge of the works of his genius, and I pointed out to him what it was that offended me in his writings. This letter served as a precedent. Years later, on re-reading the tragedy entitled *Octavia*, the memory of the letter which I had addressed to Cicero prompted me to write to Seneca also. Thereafter, and as occasion offered, I addressed letters to Varro, Vergil, and others. Some of these I have placed at the end of this work, and I hereby forewarn the reader of this fact, lest he should be perplexed at coming upon them unawares. The rest perished in that general holocaust of which I have told you above.

In the last letter of the collection *De rebus familiaribus* (XXIV, 13, likewise addressed to Socrates, and dated 1361), Petrarch refers again to the grouping together of the letters to the classical authors. He says (III, pp. 305, 306):

In ordering these letters, I have been guided entirely by their chronology, and not by their contents. [But compare Frac., 5, p. 201, on the matter of the chronology.] Nearly all of them have been arranged in the order in which they were written, with the exception, indeed, of these last letters addressed to the illustrious authors of antiquity. These I have purposely gathered together on account of their strange character and the similarity of their subject-matter. A second exception must be made in the case of the first letter, which, though written later, I have placed at the head of her companions to serve as a preface [a reference to the *Praefatio*, I, pp. 13-27].

The material embraced in these pages has been partly treated in English and to a greater extent in French (by Robinson and Rolfe, and by Develay; see Bibliography). In both cases, however, the letters chosen have been merely translated, with only the barest attempt at annotating. Even the notes of the Italian translation by Fracassetti are only such as pertain to the life of Petrarch and to those of his correspondents.

Thus much concerning the history of the text proper. The notes have been made as detailed as seemed necessary and consistent with the character of the work. Some of the quotations from the original sources, or from translations, may appear somewhat lengthy at first glance. In all instances, however, it has been deemed quite essential to reproduce in the mind of the reader the conditions and the attitude of Petrarch's mind. Only in this way do many brief expressions and pregnant allusions of Petrarch become perfectly clear.

It is a privilege and a pleasure to acknowledge my great indebtedness to two authors in particular, without whose labors the present study would have been impossible, or, at any rate, vastly more difficult: Giuseppe Fracassetti and Pierre de Nolhac. The Latin edition and the complete Italian translation of Petrarch's letters *De rebus familiaribus* (both by Fracassetti) have been absolutely indispensable; while P. de Nolhac's fascinating work has provided all the minute details concerning the actual composition and appearance of the tomes which once formed part of Petrarch's library.

All quotations from the letters are made from the Latin text and from the Italian version as published by Fracassetti. The volumes of the former are referred to by Roman numerals, those of the latter by Arabic numerals. Passages from other works of Petrarch are cited from the Basle edition of the *Opera omnia*, except the *De remediis utriusque fortunae*, for which the 1649 edition has been used. All other titles have been abbreviated in such manner as to be readily identified by consulting the Bibliography. The texts used in referring to the works of the classical authors themselves are (except when otherwise indicated) those of the Teubner series.

The number of persons interested in the absorbing period of the Italian Renaissance is increasing daily. The present study deals with only one phase of that truly wonderful period—

with the beginnings of the Classical Renaissance. But the personality of him who has justly been styled the "first modern man" is so complex, so comprehensive, that the study of any portion of his works would seem to interest not only the classical scholar, but also the student of the modern literatures, the student of Italian literature, the historian, and, finally, the large number of those who range themselves in the ranks of the Petrarchists. It is hoped that this study may make some appeal to one or to all of these classes.

The field of research on the Latin works of Petrarch is so fruitful that, during the preparation of the present volume, numerous notes have been taken with reference to Petrarch's place in politics and in religion. It is the earnest hope of the author, therefore, to pursue his researches along these lines, and to add other volumes to this preliminary study.

I. TO M. T. CICERO

(Fam., XXIV, 3)

I have read thy letters through to the end most eagerly—letters for which I had diligently searched far and wide, and which I finally came upon where I least expected. I have heard thee speak on many subjects, give voice to many laments, and waver frequently in thy opinions, O Marcus Tullius. Hitherto I knew what true counsel thou gavest to others; now, at last, I have learned to what degree thou didst prove mentor to thyself.[1]

Wherever thou mayest be, hearken in turn to this—I shall not call it advice—but lament, a lament springing from sincere love and uttered, not without tears, by one of thy descendants who most dearly cherishes thy name. O thou ever restless and distressed spirit, or, that thou mayest recognize thine own words, O thou rash and unfortunate old man![2] Why such countless enmities and rivalries bound to prove of absolutely no benefit to thee? Wherefore didst thou forsake that peaceful ease so befitting a man of thy years, and of thy vocation, and of thy station in life?[3] What false luster of glory involved thee, although weighed down with years, in the wrangles and frays proper to youths and, driving thee hither and thither through all the vicissitudes of fortune, hurried thee to an end unworthy of a philosopher? Alas, forgetful of the admonitions of thy brother,[4] forgetful of thy own numerous and wholesome precepts, like a traveler in the night didst thou bear the light in the darkness, and didst enlighten for those following thee the path on which thou thyself didst stumble most wretchedly.[5]

I forbear to speak of Dionysius; I shall make no mention of thy brother, nor of thy nephew, and, if it pleases thee, I shall pass over Dolabella too—men whom thou dost praise to the skies at one moment, and the next dost rail at in sudden wrath. Such examples of thy inconstancy may, perhaps, be excused.[6] I omit mention of Julius Caesar, even, whose oft-tested mercy proved a haven of refuge for those very persons who had assailed him. I shall say naught of the great Pompey, with whom it seemed that thou couldst accomplish anything thou didst set thy heart upon, such was the friendship between you. But what madness arrayed thee against Antony? Love for the

… Republic, I suppose thou wouldst answer. But (as thou thyself didst assert) the Republic had already been destroyed root and branch.' If, however, it was pure loyalty, if it was love of liberty that impelled thee (and we are justified in thinking thus of so great a man as thou), what meant such intimacy with Augustus? Indeed, what possible answer canst thou give to thy Brutus? "If," says he, "thou dost embrace the cause of Octavius, the evident conclusion will be, not that thou hast rid thyself of a master, but rather that thou hast sought a kindlier lord."⁸

There still remained this lamentable, finishing stroke, O Cicero, that thou shouldst speak ill of that very man, notwithstanding thy previous high praise. And on what grounds? Not because he was doing thee any wrong, but merely because he did not oppose those who were.

I grieve at thy lot, my friend; I am ashamed of thy many, great shortcomings, and take compassion on them. And so, even as did Brutus, I attach no importance to that knowledge with which I know that thou wert so thoroughly imbued.⁹ Forsooth, what boots it to instruct others, of what profit to discourse eternally on the virtues, and that too in most eloquent terms, if, at the same time, one turns a deaf ear to his own instructions? Ah, how much better had it been for a man of declining years, and especially for one devoted to studies, even as thou, to have lived his last days in the quiet of the country, meditating (as thou thyself hast said somewhere) on that everlasting life, and not on this fleeting one."¹⁰ How much better had it been never to have held office, never to have longed for triumphs,¹¹ never to have vaunted of crushing such men as Catiline. But 'tis vain indeed to talk thus. Farewell forever, my Cicero.

Written in the land of the living, on the right bank of the river Adige, in Verona, a city of Transpadane Italy, on the sixteenth day before the Kalends of Quintilis (June 16), in the thirteen hundred and forty-fifth year from the birth of that God whom thou never knewest.

Notes on *Fam.*, XXIV, 3, to Cicero

1. In 1345 Petrarch discovered in the Cathedral Library of Verona a manuscript containing the sixteen books of Cicero's letters *ad Atticum*, the three books *ad Quintum*, the two *ad Brutum*, and the apocryphal letter to Octavianus. It has been proved that he did not discover the *ad Familiares*, an honor which belongs to Coluccio Salutati (P. de Nolhac, I, pp. 222, 255).

We can readily imagine Petrarch's eagerness to possess a copy of the precious manuscript. Owing, however, to the lack of intelligent copyists, or perhaps because copyists were not admitted into the Chapter Library, Petrarch was obliged to transcribe the large volume himself, in spite of his physical debility at the time. This volume later injured Petrarch in a peculiar way, and it is interesting to hear the story from his own lips. In *Fam.*, XXI, 10, dated October 15, 1358 or 1359, he says (Vol. III, pp. 87, 88):

> But to return to Cicero, of whom I had begun to speak. You know that from early boyhood Cicero has always been dear to me, and that I have always treated him well. Now listen to what a shabby trick he has recently

played me. I possess a large volume of his letters, which I copied years ago with my own hand because the original was unintelligible to the copyists. I was very low in health at the time; but my great love for the author, the pleasure I took in reading his work, and my great eagerness to possess a copy proved superior to my physical infirmities and to the arduous task of transcription. That this volume may always be at hand, I am wont to keep it at the door of my library leaning against the door-post, where you have often seen it. The other day, while entering the room with my mind occupied on other matters (as is customary with me), it happened that the fringe of my gown became caught in the book. In falling, the volume struck my left leg just a little above the ankle. It was a very slight blow. And I, addressing it playfully, said: "What is the matter, my Cicero, why do you injure me?" Of course there was no answer. The next day as I passed the same spot, it again struck me, and again I returned it to its place jestingly. To cut a long story short, after being struck a third and a fourth time, I at last bestirred myself, and supposing that Cicero could ill brook being kept on the floor, I raised him to a higher station. By this time the skin above my ankle had been cut open by the frequent repetition of blows on the same spot, and an irritation had set in that was by no means to be despised. And yet I did despise it, thinking of the cause of the injury rather than of the injury itself. Consequently I abstained neither from bathing nor riding about, nor enjoying long walks, supposing that the wound would heal of itself in time. Gradually the injured spot began to swell, seeming offended at having been thus neglected; and then the flesh about it became discolored as if poisoned. Finally, when the pain had put an end, not only to my jesting, but also to my sleep and rest, I was forced to call in the doctors. Further neglect would have been madness, not bravery. It is now many days that they have been attending to my wound, which is no longer a laughing matter. Nor is their treatment without pain, and they say there is danger of my losing the use of the injured limb. I believe you know well enough what little faith I place in their statements one way or the other. And yet, I am weighed down with warm poultices, I am forbidden my usual food, and am constrained to an inactivity to which I am quite unaccustomed. I have grown to hate everything, and am particularly vexed at this, that I am compelled to eat dinners that are fit only for gourmands. Still, I am now on my way to recovery, so that you too will have learned of my convalescence before you had any knowledge of my accident.

This letter portrays Petrarch's love for Cicero so clearly, and gives us so vivid a picture of the human side of our author, that we cannot resist the temptation to quote from another letter written about a year later, which completes the story of the offending volume. He writes to Boccaccio (*Var.*, 25, Milan, August 18, 1360):

I greatly enjoyed the next portion of your letter, where you say that I was undeservedly injured by Cicero because (as you very neatly put it) of my too great familiarity with him. You are right: those with whom we live on the most intimate terms are the ones who most often molest us. It is a most rare and unusual thing indeed for a Hindoo to offend a Spaniard. And so it goes. Whence it happens that we are not surprised when we read of the wars of the Athenians against the Spartans, and when we witness our own wars against our neighbors. Much less do we marvel at civil wars and internal dissensions. Indeed, experience has made these so much a matter of course that it is peace and harmony rather that have become a source of wonder. If, on the other hand, we read of a Scythian king waging war with the monarchs of Egypt, or of Alexander the Macedon fighting his way into the heart of India, we are overcome by amazement, which ceases the moment we recollect the examples offered by our own history and recall the glorious and valorous expeditions of the Romans into the most distant lands. Your arguments proved to be of consolation to me, in so far as I was hurt by Cicero, with whom I most ardently desire to live on intimate terms. But I hope that I shall never be injured either by Hippocrates or by Albumazar.

But to be serious, you must know that that wound which was caused by Cicero and of which I had begun to jest, soon turned my sport to grief. Almost a year slipped by, and the condition of the wound was still going from bad to worse, while I was growing gray in the midst of pain and discomforts, doctors and poultices. Finally, when my restlessness had become intolerable and I had become tired of life, I resolved to dismiss the doctors and to await the outcome, no matter what it was, preferring to entrust myself to God and to nature rather than to those white-washers who were experimenting the tricks of their trade to my detriment. And I lived up to my resolution. I showed them the door, and placed full reliance in the aid of the Divine Preserver. The youth who waits upon me, thanks to my wound and at my expense, turned doctor. And I, remembering which of the many remedies had been of real benefit to me, made use of those only. To help nature I was careful of my diet; and so very, very gradually I am regaining the health which I lost in such short order. Now you have the story complete. Let me add one word more, that this life is an arena for toils and griefs in which I have often combated against strange mishaps, strange not in themselves, but in that they should have fallen to my lot. No one, I assure you, seeks peace more than I; no one shuns such encounters more readily than I; and never have I, hitherto, suffered such a strange calamity, whether you consider its peculiar cause, or the pain which resulted therefrom, or its long continuance. My Cicero wished to leave upon my memory an imperishable and lasting impression. I always should have remembered him, I vow; but lest I might possibly forget him, Cicero has now taken due precautions—both internal and external. And here again, what do you wish me to say? To repeat, I now perceive that life is in itself a serious work.

So much for the tome itself; now as to the inspiration received from its contents. The present letter to Cicero bears the date Verona, June 16, 1345. Hence it is clear that before leaving the city in which he had made the discovery, Petrarch had been prompted to address this letter to his favorite author. In fact we have his own testimony to this effect (see Introduction). Both this letter to Cicero and the following (*Fam.*, XXIV, 4) are mentioned again in *Fam.*, XXIV, 2, dated May 13, 1351. Petrarch here records for Pulice di Vicenza the various details of a heated discussion they had had with an old gentleman who was an idolatrous worshiper of Cicero. The story runs that Petrarch had chanced to refer to the inconstancy of Cicero, bringing utter dismay to his astonished opponents. He continues (Vol. III, pp. 258 ff.):

The situation demanded that I draw forth from my traveling-case the volume containing my correspondence. But this only heaped coals upon the fire. For, among the numerous letters to my contemporaries, there are a few which, for the sake of variety, I have addressed to the more distinguished characters of antiquity—a pleasant diversion, so to speak, from my wonted labors. The reader, if not forewarned, would be greatly astonished at finding such illustrious and ancient names mingled with those of today. Two of these letters are to Cicero himself; one of them censures his life, the second praises his genius. After you had read them to the attentive gathering, the friendly discussion was renewed with spirit. My writings found favor with some, who acknowledged that Cicero had been criticised justly. That venerable gentleman alone fought on and on with ever-increasing obstinacy. Being held captive by the splendor of the name and his love for the author, he preferred to laud even the shortcomings of Cicero, and to accept the vices of his friend together with his virtues. He did not wish to make any discrimination, lest he might seem to cast even the slightest aspersions on so praiseworthy an author. He could make no other answer to me and the rest, except to oppose to all our arguments the mere splendor of Cicero's name. Authority had driven out reason. Stretching out his hand, he exclaimed time and again: "Have mercy on my Cicero, I beg of you; be more merciful." And when asked whether Cicero could be said to have erred at all, he closed his eyes as if struck by the word, and turning away his face groaned: "Woe is me! And is it my Cicero who is thus reproved?" as if he were speaking, not of a mortal but of some deity. Hence we asked of him whether he judged Tullius a man or a god. Instantly came the reply: "A god." . . . . After long discussion, and at a late hour, we arose and departed, leaving the issue still undecided. But the last thing before separating for the evening, you exacted from me the promise to send to you a copy of those two letters the moment I should arrive at a more fixed abode—for there was no time that day. . . . . I hereby send them to you.

2. Unfortunately for the commentator, Petrarch considered as authentic the letter *ad Octavianum*, which was included in the manuscript he discovered at Verona (see n. 1). The letter is now generally considered apocryphal.

In sec. 6 occurs the phrase referred to by Petrarch: "O meam calamitosam ac praecipitem senectutem!"

3. *Rer. mem.*, i, 1, p. 393, "De ocio," has the following paragraph on Cicero:

But I am done with leaders in war. I shall now speak of M. Tullius Cicero. After countless hardships suffered in the course of his career, after such numerous dangers incurred during that most stormy consulship and in his immortal fight against unprincipled men, when the liberty of his fellow-citizens had at last been destroyed, Cicero escaped as if from a sinking ship, and, stripped of all his honors, retired into a life of seclusion. And now, in roving about from one country home to another, as he himself says (*De off.*, iii, 1, 1), he found himself alone quite frequently. But what activity in public life, I ask, was comparable to his leisure? What crowded assemblies to his isolation? Although Cicero may be pardoned for weeping bitterly over the fate of his fatherland, still from out of that solitude there spread abroad to all nations monumental products of his divine genius. Indeed, as Cicero himself says (*De off.*, iii, 1, 4), more works were struck off in that brief period than in the many years while the Republic was still standing. But his powers did not avail him in warding off his destiny. He was safe in the midst of dangers; but when at last in the haven he suffered shipwreck.

(Consult the notes of H. A. Holden, in his edition of the *De officiis*.)

4. This story is given more fully in *Rer*.

mem., iii, 3, p. 440, "De sapienter dictis vel factis, Q. Cicero":

The following proves clearly how much easier it is for a man to give good advice to others than to himself. Quintus Cicero once offered advice to Marcus Cicero, his brother, and if Marcus had accepted it, he would perhaps have died in his own bed, and his body might have been laid to rest unmutilated. The advice was that Marcus should consider carefully the wretched end of his illustrious contemporaries, and should examine closely the dangers by which he himself was beset; after which he should beware of becoming involved in strifes and conflicts which could bring no relief to the State, but which would, in the end, bring destruction upon him. Most prudent counsel indeed! For what is more fatuous than to become entangled in unending quarrels, especially when one already despairs of attaining the desired goal? Tullius himself somewhere admits that this brotherly advice was both sensible and wise. But we all know how wisely he followed it! Perchance it was the force of destiny which urged him on—a compelling force which I know not whether it was possible to resist. At any rate, such resistance must have proved very difficult. And this fact is impressed upon my mind by the subject of the following sketch.

5. Dante, *Purg.*, XXII, 64–70 (tr. by Longfellow):

> And he to him: "Thou first directedst me
> Towards Parnassus, in its grots to drink,
> And first concerning God didst me enlighten.

> Thou didst as he who walketh in the night,
> Who bears his light behind, which helps him not,
> But wary makes the persons after him,
> When thou didst say," . . . .

6. In *Fam.*, XXIV, 2 (a letter from which we have already quoted in n. 1) there are some passages fairly parallel to this one. The first is (Vol. III, p. 258):

> You may remember that Cicero's name chanced to be mentioned among us, as so often happens among learned men. This put a stop to the desultory conversation in which we had been engaged up to that time. We all became engrossed with this one topic, and nothing else but Cicero was talked of thereafter. We gathered round and each in turn sang the praises of Cicero as seemed best to him. But nothing in this world is perfect (as everyone knows), and there is no one in whom even a gentle critic cannot find just cause for censure. And so it happened that though nearly everything pleases me in Cicero—a man whom I cherish beyond all my other friends—and though I expressed admiration for his golden eloquence and divine intellect, I could not praise the fickleness of his character and his inconstancy, which I had detected in many instances.

And again, at the end of the same letter (Vol. III, p. 261), Petrarch says:

> As regards Cicero, I have known him as the best of consuls, vigilantly providing for the welfare of the State, and as a citizen who always evinced the highest love of

country. But what more? I cannot bestow praise upon the instability of his friendships, nor upon the serious disagreements arising from slight causes and bringing destruction upon him and benefit to none, nor upon a judgment which, when brought to bear upon questions of private and public affairs, did not well accord with his remarkable acumen in other directions. Above all, I cannot praise, in a philosopher weighed down with years, an inclination for wrangling which is proper to youths and utterly of no avail. Of all this, however, remember that neither you nor anyone else can be in a fit position to judge, until you will have read, and carefully, all the letters of Cicero; for it is these which gave rise to the whole discussion.

7. Petrarch has here paraphrased the words of Cicero, who employs such expressions as "maximo in discrimine res publica versatur" (*ad Br.*, i, 12, 1); "ferre praesidium labenti et inclinatae paene rei publicae" (*op. cit.*, i, 18, 2); "res existimabatur in extremum adducta discrimen" (*ibid.*, ii, 1, 1, and ii, 2, 2); "desperatam et afflictam rem publicam" (pseudo-Cic., *ad Octavianum*, 4); and "mortua re publica" (*ibid.*, 7).

8. Cic., *ad Brutum*, i, 16 (written by Brutus at Athens, May, 43 B. C.):

I have read an extract (sent to me by Atticus) of the letter which you wrote to Octavius. . . . . I am most deeply afflicted by that portion of your letter to Octavius which concerns us. You give him thanks for the welfare of the State, and—what shall I say? The conditions imposed by my present lot bring shame upon me, but still the words must be written—you suppliantly and submissively commend our safety to his mercy..... For my part I do not believe that all the gods have abandoned their protection of the Roman people to such an extent that Octavius is to be implored for the safety of any citizen whatsoever, much less, then, for that of the liberators of the entire world..... And can you, Cicero, who confess that Octavius has this power, can you still remain his friend?.... For if you are pleased with Octavius, of whom our safety is to be implored, you will seem, not to have rid yourself of a master, but rather to have sought a kindlier lord.

9. Cic., *ad Brutum*, i, 17, 5 (Brutus to Atticus, 43 B. C.): "I, in truth, attach no importance to that knowledge with which I know that Cicero was so thoroughly imbued. For what profited him to discourse, and at such great length, on his country's freedom, on dignity, on death, on exile, and on poverty?"

10. The reference is very indefinite: "in tranquillo rure senuisse, de perpetua illa, ut ipse quodam loco ais, non de hac iam exigua vita cogitantem" (Vol. III, p. 263). The passages which Petrarch had in mind may have been *De sen.*, 49: "If, however, we have something that may serve as food (so to speak)

for study and learning, there is nothing more pleasant than a leisurely old age;" and 51: "I come now to the pleasures of a country life, with which I am infinitely delighted. None of these finds an obstruction in old age, and they are pleasures which appear to me to be most nearly suited to the life of a philosopher." These two passages affirm that the sage should live a leisurely and studious old age in the country. As to meditating on the eternal life, Petrarch may have been thinking of *Acad. pr.*, ii, 127:

> By no means, however, do I hold that the studies of the natural philosophers should be excluded. Indeed, a consideration and contemplation of nature constitutes the natural food (so to speak) for our minds and talents. We are elevated thereby, and we seem to rise to a higher state of being. We disdain human affairs; and, in meditating on the higher and heavenly things, we scorn earthly matters as being small and insignificant—"cogitantesque supera atque caelestia haec nostra ut exigua et minima contemnimus."

There is a marked similarity between the two passages, both in the thought and the wording. As to the latter we must remember that Petrarch was quoting from memory and not from an open book, an inference which (we believe) may be justly drawn from his "ut ipse quodam loco ais." It is needless to add that the similarity of the two passages lies only in the letter, and that the spirit of Cicero's words was thoroughly pagan. With Petrarch, in this instance, the wish was father to the thought. Still he could not deceive himself on this point, as is evidenced by the dating of this letter. Elsewhere, too, he expresses his sincere regret, and regards Cicero as a potential Christian, if we may use the phrase. In a letter written to Neri Morando and dated October 15, 1358 or 1359, Petrarch is full and explicit. He says (*Fam.*, XXI, 10, Vol. III, pp. 85–87):

I am living in the country not far from the banks of the Adda. I know that I am not more solicitous of your welfare than you of mine. I suppose, therefore, you will be astonished at hearing how I am spending my time. You are well aware that from early boyhood of all the writers of all ages and of all races the one author whom I most admire and love is Cicero. You agree with me in this respect as well as in so many others. I am not afraid of being considered a poor Christian by declaring myself so much of a Ciceronian. To my knowledge, Cicero never wrote one word that would conflict with the principles proclaimed by Christ. If, perchance, his works contained anything contrary to Christ's doctrine, that one fact would be sufficient to destroy my belief in Cicero, and in Aristotle, too, and in Plato. For how could I place faith in man, I who should believe not even an angel, relying on the words of the Apostle who says, in the Epistle to the Galatians (1:8): "But though we, or an angel from heaven, preach any other gospel unto you than that which we have preached unto you, let him be accursed." But to return to Cicero. He frequently makes mention of the gods, following, of course, the custom of his times. He devotes an entire volume, it is true, to a discussion of the nature of the gods. If you read beneath the surface, however, you will be convinced that he does not so much pay honor to this throng of gods with their empty names, but rather exposes them to ridicule. Where he seriously expresses his own opinion Cicero asserts that there is but one God, and that He is the Prince and Ruler of the universe. I have often pointed out, both in speech and in writing, that in this respect Cicero was fully aware of the danger attending his statement of the truth. And yet, somewhere, he has clearly stated that it is not befitting a philosopher to say that there are many gods. Who, therefore, will declare Cicero hostile to the true faith, or who, because of his crass ignorance of the facts, will cast upon Cicero the opprobrium of stranger and enemy? Christ is my God; Cicero, on the other hand, is the prince of the language I use. I grant you that these ideas are widely separated, but I deny that they are at conflict one with the other. Christ is the Word, and the Virtue, and the Wisdom of God the Father. Cicero has written much on the speech of men, on the virtues of men, and on the wisdom of men—statements that are true and therefore surely acceptable to the God of truth. For since God is the living Truth, and since, as St. Augustine says, all truth proceeds from Him who is the Truth, then surely whatever truth is spoken proceeds from God. I should desire to emphasize the fact that Cicero could not have known Christ, having been called from this world shortly before Christ God became man. Oh, lamentable lot! For, considering his noble and almost divine intellect, if Cicero had seen Christ or had merely heard of His name, not only (in my opinion) would he have embraced the faith, but, with his incomparable eloquence, would most ably have spread the teachings of Christ.

11. Cic., *ad Att.*, vii, 2, 6 (50 B. C.):

Indeed, I never cherished the slightest desire for a triumph till I saw that Bibulus' most shameless letters succeeded in winning for him the decree of a thanksgiving. If he had really performed the deeds he wrote of in his letters, I should rejoice and be favorably disposed to the honor decreed him. But that honors should be showered upon him, who never advanced one step beyond the gate so long as the enemy remained on this side of the Euphrates, and that I, in whose forces lay all the hope of his army, should be denied the same honors, is an insult to both of us, to both, I say, including you too in my disgrace. Therefore I shall leave no stone unturned, and, I hope, success will crown my efforts.

II. TO M. T. CICERO
(*Fam.*, XXIV, 4)

I fear that my last letter has offended thee; for thou thyself art wont to designate as just the adage of thy friend in his Andria,[1] "Homage begets friends; truth, enemies." If my fear prove true, then accept what may in some degree soothe thy injured feelings. Let not the truth be a source of ill humor in every and all instances, I beg of thee. Men, I know, are wont to be angered at justifiable censure, and to rejoice in merited praise. Thou, indeed, O Cicero (speaking with thy leave), didst live as a man, didst speak as an orator, didst write as a philosopher. It was thy life that I found fault with, not thy intellectual powers, nor yet thy command of language. Indeed, I admire the former, and am amazed at the latter. And, moreover, in thy life I feel the lack of nothing except the element of constancy, and a desire for peace that was to have been expected of a philosopher. I look in vain for a deep-rooted antipathy to civil dissensions, to strifes utterly of no avail, considering that liberty had been crushed and that the Republic had already been mourned as dead.

Mark how different is my attitude toward thee from thine toward Epicurus on so many occasions, but especially in the *De finibus*. Whenever thou wert so inclined, thou didst praise his life and ridicule his intellect.' In thee I ridicule nothing. I take compassion, however, on the life thou didst lead; while, as I have already stated, I rejoice in thy mental abilities and in thy powers of expression. O thou great father of Roman eloquence!' Not only I, but all who take delight in the elegance of the Latin tongue render thee great thanks. Thou art the fountain-head from which we draw the vivifying waters for our meadows. We frankly confess that we have been guided by thee, assisted by thy judgments, enlightened by thy radiance; and, finally, that it was under thy auspices, so to speak, that I have gained this ability as a writer (such as it is), and that I have attained my purpose.

For the realms of poetry, however, there was at hand a second guide. The nature of the case demanded that there should be two leaders—one whom I might follow in the unencumbered ways of prose, and the other in the more restricted paths of poetry. It was necessary that there should be two men whom I should admire, respectively, for their eloquence and their song. This had needs be so. For—and I beg the kind indulgence of you both for speaking thus boldly—neither of you could serve both purposes; he could not rival thee in thy chosen field, whereas thou couldst not adapt thyself to his measured flow. I would not, indeed, have ventured to be the first to pass such criticism, even though I clearly perceived it to be true. It has already been passed before me—or, peradventure, it may have been quoted from another writer—by that great Annaeus Seneca of Cordova,[4] who, as he himself complains, was prevented from becoming acquainted with thee, not by any lapse of years, but by the fury of civil warfare.[5] He might have seen thee, but did not; withal, he was a constant admirer and worshiper both of thy works and of those of that other. Seneca, therefore, marks out the boundaries of your respective spheres, and enjoins upon each to yield to his coworker in the other field.

But I am keeping thee in suspense too long. Dost thou ask who that other guide is? Thou wilt know the man at once, if thou art merely reminded of his name. It is Publius Vergilius Maro, a citizen of Mantua, of whom thou didst prophesy such great things. For we have read that when thou, then advanced in years, hadst admired some youthful effort of his, thou didst inquire its author's name, and that, having seen the young man, thou didst express thy great delight. And then, drawing on thy unexhausted fount of eloquence, thou didst pronounce upon him a judgment which, though mingled with self-praise, was nevertheless both honorable and splendid for him: "Rome's other hope and stay."[6] This sentence, which he thus heard fall from thy lips, pleased the youth to such a degree, and was so jealously treasured in his mind, that twenty years later, when thou hadst long since ended this earthly career, he inserted it word for word into his divine poem. And if it had been thy lot to see this work, thou wouldst have rejoiced that from the first blossom thou hadst made such accurate prediction of future success. Thou wouldst, moreover, have congratulated the Latin Muses, either for leaving but a doubtful superiority to the arrogant Greek Muses, or else for winning over them a decisive victory. There are defenders for both these opinions, I grant thee. And yet, if I have come to know thee from thy works—and I feel that I know thee as intimately as if I had always lived with thee—I should say that thou wouldst have been a stern defender of the latter view, and that, just as thou hadst already granted to Latium the palm in oratory,[7] thou wouldst have done likewise in the case of poetry. I do not doubt, moreover, that thou wouldst have pronounced the *Aeneid* superior to the *Iliad*—an assertion which Propertius did not fear to make from the very beginning of Vergil's labors. For when he had meditated upon the opening lines of the inspired poem, he freely gave utterance to the feelings and hopes aroused by it in these verses:

> Yield then, ye bards of Greece, ye Romans yield,
> A mightier yet than Homer takes the field.[8]

Thus much concerning my second guide for Latin eloquence, thus much concerning Rome's other hope and stay. I come back to thee now. Thou hast already heard from me my opinions on thy life and on thy genius. Art thou desirous now of learning what lot befell thy works, of knowing in what esteem they are held either by the world in general, or else by the more learned classes? There are extant, indeed, splendid volumes—volumes which I can scarcely enumerate, much less peruse with care. The fame of thy deeds and thy works is very great, and has spread far and wide. Thy name, too, has a familiar ring to all. Very few and rare, however, are those who study thee, and for various reasons: either because of the natural perversity of the times toward such studies, or because the minds of men have become dull and sluggish, or, as I think most likely, because greed has bent their minds in an entirely different direction. Wherefore, some of thy works have (unless I am mistaken) perished in this generation, and I know not whether they will ever be recovered. Oh, how great is my grief thereat; how great is the ignominy of this age; how great the loss to posterity! It was not, I suppose, sufficiently degrading to neglect our own powers, and to bequeath to future generations no fruit of our intellects; but, worse than all else, we had to destroy the fruit also of thy labor with our cruel, our unpardonable disregard. This lamentable loss has overtaken not merely thy works, but also those of many other illustrious authors. But at present I would speak of thy writings only; and the names of those whose loss is the more regrettable are the following: *De republica, De re familiari, De re militari, De laude philosophiae,*[9] *De consolatione,* and the *De gloria.*[10] Concerning the last, however, I entertain a more or less doubtful hope of its recovery, and consequently my despair is not unqualified. Unfortunately, however, even of those books that have come down to us, there are lacking large portions. It is as if we had overcome, after a great struggle, the oblivion threatened by the sloth and inactivity of ages; but, as the price of victory, we had to mourn over our leaders, not only those to be numbered among the dead, but also the maimed and the lost. We miss this loss in many of thy works, but more especially in the *De oratore,*[11] the *Academica,* and the *De legibus*—all of which have reached us in such a fragmentary and mutilated condition that it would have been better, perhaps, had they perished altogether.

There remains still another topic. Art thou desirous of learning the present condition of Rome and of the Roman state? of knowing the actual appearance of thy fatherland, the state of harmony among its citizens, to whom the shaping of its policies has fallen, and by whose wisdom and by whose hands the reins of government are held? Art thou wondering whether or not the Danube, and the Ganges, and the Ebro, and the Nile, and the Don are still the boundaries of our empire? and whether that man has arisen among us

> The limits of whose victories
> Are ocean, of his fame the skies,

and who

> O'er Ind and Garamant extreme
> Shall stretch his reign,

as thy Mantuan friend once sang?" I feel sure that thou art most eager to hear such and similar tidings, owing to thy loyalty and the love thou didst bear the fatherland, a love remaining constant even unto death. But it is better to pass over such subjects in silence. Believe me, Cicero, if thou wert to learn of the fallen state of our country, thou wouldst weep bitter tears, be it a region of Heaven that thou inhabitest, or of Hades. Forever farewell.

From the land of the living, on the left bank of the Rhone, in Transpadane Gaul, in the same year, on the fourteenth day before the Kalends of January (at Avignon, December 19, 1345).

Notes on *Fam.*, XXIV, 4, to Cicero

1. Terence, *Andria*, i, 1, 41. Petrarch's words, "ut ipse soles dicere, quod ait familiaris tuus in Andria" (Vol. III, p. 264), are proof that he was not quoting Terence directly, but the *De amicitia*. In chap. 89 of the latter we read, "Quod in Andria familiaris meus dicit," and then follows the verse in question. The speaker is of course Laelius, of whom Terence was in fact a friend. Petrarch, therefore, has either momentarily lost sight of the speaker, or, realizing full well that Laelius is Cicero's mouthpiece, has consciously identified the two. This would, of course, make Terence a friend of Cicero; the "familiaris meus" of the *De amicitia* and the "familiaris tuus" of Petrarch both, therefore, become equivalent to "familiaris Ciceronis."

2. There is a passage in the *De finibus* in which Cicero especially contrasts the teachings of Epicurus with his life. It is ii, 80 and 81:

That philosophy which you defend, and those tenets which you have learned, and approve of, destroy friendship to the very roots, even though Epicurus does extol friendship to the skies—as we must confess. "But Epicurus himself cultivated friendships," you will say. And who, pray, is denying that he was a good and kindly man, full of sympathy for his fellow-beings? We are here discussing his intellect, not his life. We shall leave such fickleness and perversity to the Greeks, who attack with animosity all who may differ from them in their beliefs concerning truth. I must say, however, that, although he was affable in maintaining his friendships (if this be true, for I affirm nothing), yet he did not possess a keen mind. To which you will rejoin, "But he convinced many people." .... To me, indeed, the fact that Epicurus himself was a good man, and that there have been and are today many Epicureans, loyal in their friendships, consistent in their actions throughout life, serious of disposition and shaping their plans without regard to pleasure but rather through a sense of duty—to me these facts prove that the power of integrity is superior, and that of pleasure inferior. In truth, some persons live in such a way that their life confutes their words. And therefore, just as others are considered to speak better than they act, so these Epicureans (it seems) must be said to act better than they speak.

Cicero mentions the inconsistency of Epicurus in ii, 96: "Listen now .... to the dying words of Epicurus, and observe how widely his deeds and his words disagree;" and again in ii, 99: "But you will find nothing in this splendid letter of Epicurus in accord and consistent with his maxims. He refutes himself, while his theories are set at naught by his upright life."

As Petrarch says, Books I and II of the *De finibus* are crowded with favorable and adverse comments on Epicurus and his philosophy. Of the latter it will suffice to refer to i, 22, in which Cicero accuses Epicurus of being utterly wanting in logic; and to i, 26, where he denies that Epicurus can be admitted to the number of the learned.

3. Perhaps a reminiscence of Pliny, *N. H.*, vii, 30 *extr.:* "salve .... facundiae Latiarumque litterarum parens."

4. Seneca, *Contr.*, iii, *praef.* 8.

5. Seneca, *Contr.*, i, *praef.* 11.

6. *Aen.*, xii, 168. Donatus, *Vita Verg.*, XI, 41 (p. 60 R, through *pronuntiarentur* only):

> The publication of the Bucolics was attended by such great success that they were frequently recited, even by actors on the stage. Cicero once heard some of the verses, and his keen judgment at once perceived that they were written in no common vein. So he ordered the eclogue to be recited from the beginning; and after listening attentively to the very end, he exclaimed, "Rome's other hope and stay;" as if he himself had been the first hope of the Latin tongue, and Maro were to be the second. These words Maro afterward inserted in the *Aeneid*.

This version does not mention Cicero's inquiry as to the author of the verses he admired ("quaesivisses auctorem"), nor their meeting ("eumque .... vidisses") nor the fact that his exclamation was flattering both to himself and to Vergil ("cum propria quidem laude permixtum"). Servius' version, however, does include these three elements, and hence he is to be considered Petrarch's source. He writes (*ad Ecl.*, vi, 11):

> It is said that Vergil's reading of this eclogue (vi) was received with great favor; so much so, indeed, that when later Cytheris the courtesan (whom Vergil calls Lycoris in the last eclogue) sang it in the theater, Cicero in amazement inquired who the author of it was ("cuius esset requireret"). And when at last Cicero had seen him ("eum .... vidisset"), he is said to have exclaimed, in praise of both himself and that other ("et ad suam et ad illius laudem"), "Rome's other hope and stay"—a phrase which Vergil afterward applied to Ascanius, as the commentators relate.

This version was one which would especially appeal to Petrarch; for, as P. de Nolhac justly observes (I, p. 125), it represents Petrarch's two literary idols as having been personally acquainted with each other.

And, finally, in favor of the Servian origin is the fact that in Donatus the entire story appears in the interpolated version of the *Vita*, and it is doubtful whether Petrarch was acquainted with this longer version (Sabbadini, *Rend. del R. Ist. Lomb.*, [1906], p. 198). The interpolated text of the *Vita* has, in fact, been traced only as far back as the beginning of the fifteenth century; the date temporarily assigned to it is 1400–20 (Sabbadini, "La 'Vergilii Vita' di Donato," *Studi Italiani di Filologia Classica*, Vol, V, 1897, pp. 384–88).

7. Cicero, however, is much more guarded in his statement than we would infer from the words of Petrarch; *Tusc.*, i, 3, 5: "Then came the Lepidi, Carbo, and the Gracchi, and so many great orators after them down to our own times, that we were very little, if at all, inferior to the Greeks."

8. Translation, by Ch. R. Moore (p. 73), of Propertius, ii, 34*b*, 65, 66 (*rec.* Aem. Baehrens, Teubner, 1880) or ii, 34, 65, 66 (H. E. Butler, 1905).

There is abundant proof that Petrarch was acquainted with Propertius (P. de Nolhac, I, pp. 170–72). Still, from the few indirect references to this author, one is inclined to believe that Petrarch here (as elsewhere) is drawing upon the *Life* by Donatus for biographical information on Vergil. And in fact the Propertian couplet seems to derive from Donatus, *Vita Verg.*, XII, 45 (p. 61R), the "operis fundamenta" and "asseverare non timuit" of Petrarch (Vol. III, p. 266), corresponding, respectively, to the "Aeneidos vixdum coeptae" and "non dubitaverit sic praedicare" of Donatus. In commenting upon this famous distich, H. Nettleship says ("Vergil," in *Classical Writers* [New York, 1880], p. 86): "Propertius and Ovid saw at once what was in Vergil. Of the *Aeneid* Propertius said 'something greater than the *Iliad* is coming to the birth.'" (Cf. *Ancient Lives of Vergil* [Oxford, 1879], p. 67.) Comparetti, however, has chosen a different course in his *Vergil in the Middle Ages* (tr. by Benecke, 1895). On p. 3, after stating that the Romans confessed Vergil's inferiority to Homer, he continues in a footnote:

> The exaggerations of a few enthusiasts must not be reckoned at more than their real value. How great a part of the "Nescio quid maius nascitur Iliade" of Propertius was due to his friendship with Vergil becomes clear when we compare with it the praises he lavishes on the *Thebaid* of another friend, Ponticus.

9. In a large tome containing Cicero's writings, and supposed to have belonged to Petrarch,

there occurred the rubric "de laude ac defensione philosophiae, introducens Lucullum loquentem ad Hortensium, liber primus incipit." Petrarch, misled by this heading, had been of the opinion that the work following was the *Hortensius*. As a matter of fact, it was book ii of the *Academica Priora*, which has the separate subtitle "Lucullus" (P. de Nolhac, I, pp. 228, 244 ff.). He labored under this delusion for some time, until in reading St. Augustine he met citations from the real *Hortensius*, which of course he could not verify in his supposed *Hortensius*. Finally he received from Marco Barbato da Sulmona, whom he had met in 1341 at Naples, a manuscript containing a work inscribed *Academica*. Investigation quickly showed him that this work and his supposed *Hortensius* were one and the same. But he was unwilling to relinquish the idol he had worshiped so long. Doubts still remained. On his visit to Naples in 1343, however, he identified once and for all the work in his own manuscript; and on his return he entered the following note abreast of the heading: "This title, though common, is nevertheless a false one. This is not the *De laude philosophiae*, but the last two of the four books of the *Aca-*

demica." The present letter to Cicero was written in 1345, two years after the correction of his error; hence Petrarch rightly places the *De laude philosophiae (sive Hortensius)* in the catalogue of lost books.

The closing statement of Petrarch's postilla needs a few words of explanation. The fragment which he possessed constituted book ii of the *Ac. priora*. Petrarch supposed that he had not one, but two books. The deception was due to an arbitrary division in his manuscript at the words "Hortensius autem vehementer" (*Ac. pr.*, ii, 63). Still another error existed. Petrarch thought that his fragment was part of the second edition of the *Academica* in four books—the *Posteriora* dedicated to Varro, of whose existence he had learned from the letters to Atticus (cf. xiii, 13) which he had discovered earlier in the same year.

10. Every biography relates how Petrarch gave in loan to his teacher, Convennole (or Convenevole) da Prato, a manuscript containing the *De gloria* of Cicero; and how the schoolmaster, in an hour of extreme need, pawned the volume, which could never again be found in spite of Petrarch's constant search for it. The story as we have it is told by Petrarch him-

self, in a letter written in 1374, the very last year of his life (*Sen.*, xvi, 1).

Modern scholarship has cast doubts upon the tale. P. de Nolhac discusses the question thoroughly in Vol. I, pp. 260-68. His explanation of the evolution of the idea which possessed Petrarch is the following.

In his youth Petrarch must have read in the lost volume some beautiful passages on glory—passages which remained more or less firmly fixed in his mind. In later years, when his scholarship broadened, he learned of a separate work by Cicero on the subject of glory; and, questioning his memory, the remembrance of those passages became so clear and distinct that he began to imagine he had really possessed the *De gloria* in the volume unfortunately loaned to his schoolmaster. The hope arose that he might some day find the volume again. It was while in this stage that he wrote the present letter (1345), saying that he entertained a more or less doubtful hope of its recovery and that his despair was not unqualified. His regret increased with the years. By dreaming of his hoped-for recovery of the manuscript, by discussing it with his friends year after year, Petrarch finally, as so often results from the frequent repetition of a story, persuaded himself that he had at one time been the actual possessor of the *De gloria*. Hence it was that, writing thirty years later, in 1374, when his mind was losing its firm grip on facts, and when he was tottering on the brink of the grave, the unfulfilled hope for a thing long desired turned into a regret for a thing actually lost (*op. cit.*, p. 266).

11. Petrarch was mistaken in placing the *De oratore* among the fragmentary works. In the large tome already referred to, there followed hard upon the heels of the *De oratore* what is now known as the *Orator*. The latter did not, however, bear a separate title, and consequently Petrarch considered it as a fourth book to the *De oratore*. Moreover, this pseudo-fourth book had a large lacuna, for it began only with the words "(aliquan) toque robustius" (sec. 91); and the lacuna being clearly indicated, Petrarch unavoidably thought the *De oratore* incomplete (P. de Nolhac, I, pp. 228-30, 242). To be correct he should have written *Orator* instead of *De oratore*. But even this would scarcely have mended matters; for, not being aware of the separate existence of these two works, Petrarch was wont to cite passages from

one and the other, employing the indiscriminate title *Orator* (*ibid.*, pp. 253, 254).

After this enumeration of the lost and fragmentary works, it will be interesting to know with how many writings of Cicero Petrarch was really acquainted at this time. Fortunately for our purpose, he writes to Lapo da Castiglionchio in 1352, describing to him the beauty and quiet of his retreat at Vaucluse, and the reading with which he occupied all his time. The letter in full—*Fam.*, xii, 8:

> According to my custom, I fled recently from the turmoil of the city that is so odious to me, and betook myself to my Helicon across the Alps. I brought with me your Cicero, who was greatly astonished at the beauty of these new regions and who confessed that never—not even when in his own retreat at Arpinum—had he (to use his own phrase) been surrounded by cooler streams than when with me at the Fountain of the Sorgue. I suppose that when, long ago, he visited Narbonne, he did not observe this country. And yet, if we are to believe Pliny, this district formed part of the province of Narbonne; and, according to the present division, it is part of the province of Arles. Whatever be the truth concerning the geographical division of the provinces, one thing is certain, that the Fountain of the Sorgue is most renowned, second neither to the Campanian Nymph nor to the Sicilian Arethusa. This soothing, quiet, peaceful country, and this delightsome retreat are situated to one side

of the public highway, to the right of one seeking it, to the left of him returning therefrom. I have thus minutely described its site lest you might wonder that Cicero, while traveling in these parts so long ago, failed to notice this sequestered spot, delightful as it is. No mere passer-by has ever discovered it. No one has ever reached it except purposing to do so through certain knowledge of its existence, drawn to the spot by the beauty of the Fountain, or by his desire for repose and study. And how unusual this is you will soon realize if you consider on the one hand the great scarcity of poets, and on the other the multitude of those who have not even a smattering of the liberal arts. Cicero therefore seems to rejoice and to be eager to remain in my company. We have now passed ten quiet and restful days together here. Here only, and in no other place outside of Italy, do I breathe freely. In truth, study has this great virtue, that it appeases our desires for a life of solitude, mitigates our aversion for the vulgar herd, tenders us sought-for repose even in the midst of the thickest crowds, instils in us many noble thoughts, and provides us with the fellowship of most illustrious men even in the most solitary forests.

My companion was attended by a numerous and distinguished gathering. Not to mention those of Greek birth, the Romans present were Brutus, Atticus, and Herennius, all of them rendered still more honorable by their presence in the works of Cicero [*Epistolae ad Brutum, Atticum, Auctor ad Herennium*]. Marcus Varro, also, was present, that most learned of all men, with whom Cicero strolled in the villa of the Academics [*Academica;* cf. n. 9.]; and Cotta, and Velleius, and Lucilius

Balbus, with whom he so keenly discussed the nature of the gods [*De natura deorum*]; and Nigidius and Cratippus, with whom he investigated the secrets of nature, the origin of the universe and its composition [*Timaeus, sive de universo*]. We had with us, moreover, Quintus Cicero, with whom he treated of the subject of divination and laws [*De divinatione, De legibus*]; and his own son, Marcus Cicero, to whom (when not as yet degenerated) he addressed his *De officiis*, pointing out to him what was honorable, and what expedient, and the conflict between the two. Sulpicius, Crassus, and Antonius— all very eloquent orators—formed part of our company, together with whom he explored the most hidden secrets of the art of oratory [*De oratore*]. Cato the Elder, too, was with us, whom Cicero made the spokesman in his praise of Old Age [*De senectute*]. Of our band were also Lucius Torquatus, Marcus Cato Uticensis and Marcus Piso, with whom, after a most painstaking discussion, he set down his theory of the "summum bonum" [*De finibus*]. Furthermore, we had the orator Hortensius, and Epicurus, the former represented in Cicero's praise of philosophy [cf. n. 9.], the latter in his attack on a life of pleasure. With Laelius he outlined the course of true friendship [*De amicitia*], with Scipio the government of the "ideal State." I shall not prolong my enumeration *in infinitum;* I shall merely add that among the Roman citizens there mingled many foreign rulers whom Cicero defended with his divine powers of oratory. However, not to omit those whose presence was due to your little volume, my friend, I shall mention Milo whom Cicero defended, and Laterensis whom he so fearlessly attacked [*Pro Plancio*], and Sulla, for whom he pleaded [*Pro Corn. Sulla*], and Pompey, whom he so highly praised [*De imperio Pompei*]. With such men and others as my companions, my stay in the country has been a quiet, peaceful, and happy one. Would that it had continued longer. But alas, they have once again laid their claws upon me, and have once again dragged me to the Hades whence I am writing you this letter. I have been so busily engaged since then that my young attendant has found no time whatever for transcribing your volume, nor have I had any opportunity of returning it to you. I trust that this will not be necessary until I can return it to you in Italy personally. I am promising myself an early return, provided I can induce our friend Forese to visit the above-mentioned Helicon the moment he is not so overwhelmingly occupied by his affairs. And I shall insist upon his visit in order that if at any time hereafter fate, or the love of change, or the desire to escape ennui will compel me to return—not to this city (whither, if I can help it, I shall never return), but to my Transalpine retreat—I shall be more readily pardoned by my friends in Italy by calling upon the testimony of so important a witness. Farewell.

12. *Aeneid* i, 287, and vi, 794, 795, tr. by Conington (ed. 1900), pp. 13 and 210.

III. TO L. ANNAEUS SENECA
(*Fam.*, XXIV, 5)

On another occasion, O Seneca, I begged and obtained the pardon of a great man indeed.¹ I should desire similar indulgence on thy part, if I express myself more sharply than is quite consistent with the reverence due to thy calling and to the peace of the grave. Whosoever has seen that I have not spared Marcus Cicero—whom (upon thy authority²) I called the bright luminary and fountain-head of Latin eloquence—will surely have no just cause for indignation because in continuing to speak the truth, I shall not spare thee or anyone else. I derive great enjoyment from speaking with you, O illustrious characters of antiquity. Each succeeding age has suffered your works to remain in great neglect; but our own age is quite content, in its ignorance, with a dearth that has become extraordinary. For my part, I daily listen to your words with more attention than can be believed; and so, perchance, I shall not be considered impertinent in desiring you in your turn to listen to me once.

I am fully aware that thou art to be numbered

among those whose names are illustrious. Were I unable to gather this from any other source, I should still learn it from a great foreign authority. Plutarch, a Greek and the tutor of Emperor Trajan, in comparing the renowned men of his country with those of ours, opposed Marcus Varro to Plato and Aristotle (the former of whom the Greeks call divine, the latter inspired), Vergil to Homer, and Marcus Tullius to Demosthenes. He finally dared to discuss even the vexed question of military leaders, in the treatment of which he was not hampered by the respect due to his great pupil. In one department of learning, however, he did not blush to acknowledge that the genius of the Greeks was distinctly inferior, saying that he knew not whom to place on a par with thee in the field of moral philosophy.[3] Great praise this, especially from the mouth of a man proud of his race, and a startling concession, seeing that he had opposed his Alexander the Macedon to our Julius Caesar.

I cannot explain why it is, but often the most perfect mold of either mind or body is marred by some serious blemish of nature, which speaks in such various language. It may be that our common mother denies perfection to mankind (the more so, indeed, the nearer we seem to approach it), or else that among so much that is beautiful even the slightest defect becomes noticeable. That which in a face of average beauty might be considered an engaging and attractive mark becomes a positively ugly scar on features of surpassing beauty. The juxtaposition of contradictory things always sheds light upon doubtful points.

And yet do thou, O venerable sir and (according to Plutarch) incomparable teacher of moral philosophy, do thou review with me calmly the great error of thy life. Thou didst fall upon evil days, in the reign of the most savage ruler within the memory of man.[4] Though thyself a peaceful mariner, thou didst guide thy bark, heavily laden as it was with the most precious goods, toward an unspeakably dangerous and tempestuous reef. But, I ask, why didst thou tarry there? Was it, perhaps, that thou mightest the better evince thy masterly skill in so stormy a sea? None but a madman would have thus chosen. To be sure, it is the part of a brave man to face danger resolutely, but not that of a wise man to seek it. Were the prudent man to be given a free choice, he would so live that there would never be need of bravery; for nothing would ever happen to him that would compel him to make any call upon it. The wise man will rather (as the name implies) check all excessive demonstrations of joy, and confine his desires within proper bounds. But since the accidents of life are countless, and since our best-laid plans are many times undone thereby, we must oppose to mad fortune an unconquerable fortitude, not from choice (as I have already said), but in obedience to the hard, inexorable laws of necessity.

But shall I not seem to have lost my senses if I continue to preach on virtue to the great teacher of morality, and if I labor to prove that which can by no manner of means be confuted, namely, that it was folly to remain among the shoals? I leave it for thee to judge—nay, for anyone who has learned to sail the sea of life even tolerably well. If thy object was to reap glory from the very difficulty of thy situation, I answer that it would have been most glorious to extricate thyself therefrom and to bring thy ship in safety to some port. Thou didst see the sword hanging perpetually over thy head, yet didst fear not, nor didst thou take any step to escape from such a perilous existence. And thou shouldst have, especially since thou must have realized that thy death was to be that most wretched of all deaths—one entirely devoid of advantage to others and of glory to thyself. Thou hadst fallen, O pitiable man, into the hands of one who had the power to do what he willed,[5] but who willed nothing except it were most vile. At the very beginning of thy intimate acquaintance with him thou wert warned by a startling dream,[6] and thereafter, whenever thou wert closely observant, thou didst discover many traits that proved thy fears to be well grounded. What, therefore, could induce thee to remain so long a member of his household? What couldst thou have in common with such an inhuman and bloodstained pupil? or with courtiers so repugnant to thy very nature? Thou mayest answer: "I wished to flee, but could not;" and thou mayest adduce as a plea that verse of Cleanthes which thou art wont to quote in its Latin form:

Fate leads the willing and drags the unwilling.[7]

Thou mayest, moreover, assert that thou didst desire to renounce thy life of ease, to break the toils in which wealth had enmeshed thee, and, even though in utter destitution, to escape from such a whirlpool. This defense was known also to the ancient historians, and I who follow in their footsteps was not able to pass it over in silence.[8] But if I concealed my innermost thoughts when defending thee in public, dost thou suppose that now, when my words are addressed directly to thee, I shall suppress what my indignation and love of truth urge me to say? Come now, approach nearer, that no stranger may overhear on becoming aware that time has not robbed us of a knowledge of thy doings.

We have (thou must know) a most trustworthy authority, one who, though writing of men in the highest station, was influenced neither by fear nor favor, Suetonius Tranquillus. And dost thou know what he says? That thou didst discourage Nero's reading of the ancient orators in order that thou mightest retain him the longer as an admirer of thine own writings.[9] In other words, thou didst strive with might and main to be dear to one to whom thou shouldst have found some means of becoming an object of sovereign contempt and derision, by either feigning to have, or else really possessing, an irrepressible tongue. Am I not right? The first cause of all thy misery was the shallowness of thy aim, not to say its worthlessness. Though weighed down with years, thou didst pursue the elusive phantom of glory entirely too joyously, I might almost say childishly. Let us grant for the moment that it was the advice of another, or an error on thy part, or even fate that made thee the teacher of that ungovernable man—for in seeking to excuse our own faults we are wont to lay the blame on fate. But it was *thy* fault that thou didst remain his sponsor. Thou canst not accuse fortune; thy prayers were answered and thou obtainedst that which thou hadst so ardently longed for.

But how was it all to end? Ah, thou wretched man! Since thou hadst endeared thyself to that wild youth to such an extent as to render it impossible for him to leave thee at will, shouldst thou not at least have borne with greater resignation the yoke which thou hadst assumed of thine own accord?[10] Shouldst thou not at least have refrained from branding the name of thy master with everlasting infamy?[11] Didst thou not know that tragedy is the most serious of all compositions, as Naso says?[12] And we all know how biting, how virulent, and how vehement is the tragedy that thou didst write against him."[13] Receive my words in good part, O Seneca, and be calm, for the more impatiently one listens to the truth the more deeply is he wounded by it. Unless perchance I am wronging thee, and the contention of some be true, that the author of those tragedies is not thou, but another bearing the same name. For the Spaniards assert both that Cordova produced two Senecas,[14] and that the name of that tragedy (written against Nero) is *Octavia*. In this play there is a passage that gives rise to the suspicion of authorship.[15] If we accept the conclusions drawn therefrom, thou wilt be entirely acquitted of having written the tragedy to avenge the burden of thy yoke. As far as style is concerned, that other author (whoever he is) is by no means thy inferior, although he is later than thou in time and far behind thee in reputation. The more inadequate is the attack on infamous conduct, the weaker is the intellectual power of the writer. Indeed, beyond the attack on Nero there is (in my opinion) no other excuse for the writing of that much-discussed play. And the attack must be inadequate in this case, for I realize that no bitterness of either thought or expression could be quite commensurate with the abominable deeds of that man—if he be worthy the name of man.

Consider, however, whether it was proper for thee to write of him as thou didst, when the relationship between you was that of subject and sovereign, subordinate and superior, teacher and pupil. Was it fitting that thou shouldst write thus of him whom it was thy custom to flatter, or rather (not to mince matters) by flattering, deceive? Re-read the books which thou didst dedicate to him on the subject of Mercy;[16] recollect the sentiments expressed in the volume which thou didst address to Polybius on Consolation; finally, run over thy other works, the fruit of many sleepless nights, provided that the waters of Lethe have not wiped out all memory of them. Do as I say, and (I am sure) thou wilt be ashamed of the praises thou didst lavish upon thy pupil. I for one cannot comprehend thy effrontery in penning such words of such a man; I cannot read them without a sense of shame. But thou wilt have recourse to the customary defense, I know. Thou wilt adduce the youth of the prince and his disposition, which gave promise of much better results; and thou wilt endeavor to defend the error of thy choice by his sudden and unexpected change in life."[17] As if these arguments were unknown to us! But consider this, how utterly inexcusable it was that a few, unimportant acts of a charlatan prince, and his murmured hypocritical phrases on duty, should have warped the mind and judgment of a man of thy discretion, thy years, thy experience in life, and thy learning. Tell me, pray, what deed of Nero pleased thee? I mean of course before he plunged headlong into the abyss of disgraceful crimes—that earlier period whose deeds some historians record (to use their own words)[18] with no reproof, others with no inconsiderable amount of praise. Which of them, I ask, pleased thee? Was it his fondness for contending in the chariot-race,[19] or for playing on the cithern? We read, in fact, that he diligently applied himself to these pursuits; that at first he practiced in secret, in the presence of his slaves and the squalid poor only, but that later he performed even in public, and, though a monarch, drove his chariot in sight of all Rome like an ordinary charioteer; and that, posing as a pre-eminent player, he worshiped the cithern presented to him as if it had been a divinity.[20] At last, elated at these successes, and as if not content with the critical acumen of the Italians, he visited Achaia, and, puffed up by the adulation of the art-loving Greeks, declared that only they were worthy of being his listeners."¹ Ridiculous monster, savage beast!"² Or, perhaps, didst thou consider the following a sure omen of a good and conscientious ruler, that he consecrated on the Capitol his first growth of beard, the first molting of his inhuman face?"³

These surely are acts of thy Nero, O Seneca, and acts performed by him at an age when the historians still reckoned him among human beings, and when thou didst strive to set him among the gods by commendations worthy neither of the one praising nor the one praised. Indeed, thou didst not hesitate to rank him above that best of rulers, the deified Augustus."⁴ I do not know whether thou art ashamed of this; I am. But I suppose thou didst deem Nero's deeds worthy of greater praise, in that he tortured the Christians, a truly holy and harmless sect, but (as it seemed to him and to Suetonius who tells the story) guilty of embracing a new and baneful superstition."⁵ Nero had now become the persecutor and the most bitter enemy of all righteousness. In all seriousness, however, I do not entertain such an evil opinion of thee, wherefore I wonder all the more at thy earlier resolutions. And naturally so, because the youthful deeds of Nero were too pitiful and vain, whereas his persecution was execrable and frightful. This must have been thy opinion, for in one of thy letters to the apostle Paul thou didst not only intimate, but actually declare it.[6] Nor, I feel sure, couldst thou have thought otherwise, once thou hadst given a willing ear to his holy and heavenly teachings, and hadst embraced a friendship so divinely held out to thee. Would that thou hadst been more steadfast and that thou hadst not in the end been torn away from him! Would that, together with that messenger of the Truth, thou hadst chosen to die for the sake of that same Truth, for the promised reward in heaven, and in honor of that great apostle!

The impulse of my subject, however, has taken me too far, and I perceive that I have begun my sowing too late to entertain any hopes of a good crop. So farewell forever.

Written in the land of the living, in Cisalpine Gaul, between the left bank of the greedy Enza and the right bank of the bridge-shattering Parma, on the Kalends of Sextilis (August 1) in the year from the birth of Him whom I am uncertain whether thou didst know or not, the thirteen hundred and forty-eighth.

Notes on *Fam.*, XXIV, 5, to Seneca

1. A reference to the opening lines of the preceding letter, *Fam.*, XXIV, 4.

2. Seneca, *Ep.*, 40, 11: "Cicero quoque noster, a quo Romana eloquentia exsiluit, gradarius fuit;" (cf. Seneca, *Contr.*, i, *praef.* 6). Petrarch refers to that passage in his second letter to Cicero, *Fam.* XXIV, 4, beginning with the words, "O Romani eloquii summe parens" (Vol. III, p. 264).

3. The only passages in which Plutarch mentions Seneca are "De cohibenda ira," *Moralia*, Vol. III, p. 201, ll. 16-23, and "Galba," chap. XX, *init.* In neither of these is there any praise of the philosopher. Moreover, it is useless to search through the works of Plutarch, because Petrarch was acquainted with not a single one of his works. Hence the statement made in the Lemaire edition, Vol. CIV, p. xlviii, that "Petrarch had access to several ancient works which are absolutely lost to us," cannot apply in this case at least. Petrarch, however, was acquainted with the "Institutio Traiani" (a Latin fabrication), the authenticity of which is today disputed. P. de Nolhac has pointed

this out (II, p. 122), and shows that Petrarch actually refers to this work by name in the *Remedium*, I, 81. And even closer acquaintance is revealed in *Fam.*, XXIV, 7, where Petrarch writes to Quintilian that the indiscretions of his wards (Domitian's grandnephews) were made to detract from his fair name (Vol. III, p. 280). These words are quoted verbatim from the "Institutio Traiani" (*Moralia*, Vol. VII, p. 183); and in the same passage Plutarch makes a precisely similar reference to Seneca and to Socrates. The grouping of these three names is somewhat contradictory to the statement which Petrarch makes in the present letter.

4. Seneca, *Octavia*, 441-46 (tr. by E. I. Harris):

> SENECA. The garnered vices of so many years
> Abound in us, we live in a base age
> When crime is regnant, when wild lawlessness
> Reigns and imperious passion owns the sway
> Of shameless lust; the victress luxury
> Plundered long since the riches of the world
> That she might in a moment squander them.

5. Dante, *Inf.*, III, 94-96 (tr. by Longfellow):

> And unto him the Guide: "Vex thee not Charon;
> It is so willed there where is power to do
> That which is willed; and farther question not."

It borders on the sacrilegious, however, to make this reference, when we consider the One meant in the verses of Dante.

6. Suet., *Nero*, 7. This passage is the source also of *Rer. mem.*, IV, 4, *De somniis*, in which (p. 474) Petrarch gives the story of this dream at greater length.

Annaeus Seneca (a Roman senator at the time) was chosen by Emperor Claudius as tutor for the young Nero, who then gave hopeful signs of a good and kindly nature. The very next night Seneca is said to have dreamt that he had as his pupil C. Caligula, whose most horrible cruelty had long since met with a fitting end. Seneca was awakened, and had good cause for wondering greatly. But not much later the humor of Nero changed, or, to put it more correctly, it revealed itself, and his heart became entirely devoid of feelings of gentleness. All wonder was dispelled. Nero was a second Caligula, so much like him had he become. Nay! Caligula himself seemed somehow to have returned from the regions of the dead. And now I shall return to dreams had by emperors.

7. Seneca, *Ep.*, 107, 11: "Ducunt volentem fata, nolentem trahunt." Cf. also *Dial.*, i, *De Providentia*, 5, 7: "Fata nos ducunt." In *Ep.*, 107, 10, Seneca distinctly says that he has translated the verses from the Greek of Cleanthes. These four verses, with their trans-

lation, can be found in Ramage, *Familiar Quotations from Latin Authors*, p. 671.

8. In *Rer. mem.*, III, 3, p. 441, quoted in full in note 10 below.

9. Suet., *Nero*, 52. In this instance, as in all references to Suetonius in this letter, Petrarch follows his original very closely; indeed, quotes him almost verbatim (cf. Frac., Vol. III, p. 271).

10. Seneca, *Octavia*, 388–407 (tr. by E. I. Harris):

> SENECA. I was content, why hast thou flattered me,
> O potent Fortune, with thy treacherous smiles?
> Why hast thou carried me to such a height,
> That lifted to the palace I might fall
> The farther, look upon the greater crimes?
> Ah, happier was I when I dwelt afar
> From envy's stings, among the rugged cliffs
> Of Corsica, where my free spirit knew
> Leisure for study. Ah, how sweet it was
> To look upon the sky, th' alternate change
> Of day and night, the circuit of the earth,
> The moon, the wandering stars that circle her,
> And the far-shining glory of the sky,
> Which when it has grown old shall fall again
> Into the night of chaos,—that last day
> Has come, which 'neath the ruin of the skies
> Shall bury this vile race. A brighter sun,
> Newborn, shall bring to life another race,
> Like that the young world knew, when Saturn ruled
> In the high heavens.

As a comment on this passage, we may repeat, with Dante (*Inf.*, V, 121-23, tr. by Longfellow):

> There is no greater sorrow
> Than to be mindful of the happy time
> In misery.

At the time of his exile in Corsica, however, Seneca did not hold quite the same opinion of his life on that island, and wrote the *Consolatio ad Polybium*, full of flattery of Emperor Claudius, mainly to effect his recall.

Petrarch dwells upon the fate of Seneca also in *Rer. mem.*, III, 3, p. 441:

> In a certain tragedy (the *Octavia*) Annaeus Seneca deplores in strong and magnificent lines his return from exile in the island of Corsica, where he had been living in sweet leisure, in most welcome peace of mind, and free to pursue what studies he pleased. He shuddered at the daily increasing ungodliness of Nero, at the envy of the courtiers which enveloped everything, and often sought to escape. But fearing that his riches would prove his undoing and would overwhelm him like the waves of the sea, he surrendered them all. A wise precaution, truly. For it is the part of a wise sailor to hurl his treasures into the tempestuous sea, that he may escape by swimming, even though entirely destitute. And similarly expedient is it for him who fears death at the hands of the enemy to sacrifice calmly the limb by which he is fettered, in order that, though maimed, he may effect his escape. No one, indeed, reproves Seneca for

remaining against his will in that hotbed of crimes. He left no stone unturned to escape the crisis which he foresaw. But an unswerving destiny blocked this man too, and at the very moment when success seemed about to crown his efforts. Fate did not permit him to pass, until that inhuman and perjured emperor, who had often sworn to him that he would die sooner than do him an injury, shortened the closing years of his aged teacher, not with an untimely, but with an irreverent and an undeserved death.

11. Seneca, *Octavia*, 89-102 (tr. by E. L. Harris):

OCTAVIA. Ah, sooner could I tame
The savage lion or the tiger fierce,
Than that wild tyrant's cruel heart, he hates
Those sprung of noble blood, he scorns alike
The gods and men. He knows not how to wield
The fortune his illustrious father gave
By means of basest crime. And though he blush,
Ungrateful, from his cursed mother's hands
To take the empire, though he has repaid
The gift with death, yet shall the woman bear
Her title ever, even after death.

Octavia, 240-56:

OCTAVIA. With the fierce leader's breath the very air
Is heavy. Slaughter new the star forebodes
To all the nations that this vile king rules.
Typhoeus whom the parent earth brought forth,
Angered by Jupiter, was not so fierce;
This pest is worse, the foe of gods and men;

He from their temples drives th' immortal gods,
The citizens he exiles from their land,
He took his brother's life, his mother's blood
He drank, he sees the light, enjoys his life,
Still draws his poisonous breath! Ah, why so oft,
Mighty creator, throwest thou in vain
Thy dart from royal hand that knows not fear?
Why sparest thou to slay so foul an one?
Would that Domitian's son, the tyrant harsh,
Who with his loathsome yoke weighs down the earth,
Who stains the name Augustus with his crimes,
The bastard Nero, might at last endure
The penalty of all his evil deeds.

Octavia, 630–43:

AGRIPPINA. Ah, spare, revenge is thine! I do not ask
For long; th' avenging goddess has prepared
Death worthy of the tyrant, coward flight,
Lashes, and penalties that shall surpass
The thirst of Tantalus, the heavy toil
Of Sisyphus, the bird of Tityus,
The flying wheel that tears Ixion's limbs.
What though he build his costly palaces
Of marble, overlays them with pure gold?
Though cohorts watch the armored chieftain's gates,
Though the world be impoverished to send
Its wealth to him, though suppliant Parthians kneel
And kiss his cruel hand, though kingdoms give
Their riches, yet the day shall surely come
When for his crimes he will be called to give
His guilty soul; when, banished and forlorn,
In need of all things, he shall give his foes
His life-blood.

12. Ovid, *Tristia*, ii, 381: "Omne genus scripti gravitate tragoedia vincit."

13. The *Octavia*. See below, n. 15.

14. Martial, i, 61, 7 and 8 (Fried.):

    Duosque Senecas, unicumque Lucanum
        Facunda loquitur Corduba.

And yet these lines never suggested to Petrarch the distinction between Seneca the rhetorician and Seneca the philosopher.

15. Teuffel, par. 290: "The praetexta entitled Octavia is certainly not by Seneca." With this compare par. 290, n. 7, which gives a discussion of the above, and the bibliography. Teuffel says that l. 630 of the *Octavia* describes the death of Nero, and consequently could not have been written by Seneca, who died some years earlier. It is these lines to which Petrarch refers when he says: "In this play there is a passage that gives rise to the suspicion of authorship."

16. The *De clementia*, having been written in 55–56 A.D., and dedicated to Nero, naturally contains numerous passages in praise of that emperor. We shall choose a few from the first book. *De clementia*, i, 1, 5–8:

This, O Caesar, you can boldly assert; that you have most diligently cherished everything entrusted to your faithful care, and that no harm has been plotted against the State by you either through open violence or through stealth. You have aspired to that rarest of praise, hitherto granted to none of our emperors—the praise of being thoroughly upright. You have not labored in vain. Your matchless virtues have not found ungrateful and spiteful appraisers. We render thee thanks. No one person has ever been as dear to a single man as you are to the entire Roman people. . . . . But you have shouldered a heavy burden; you have assumed a great responsibility. No one now speaks of the deified Augustus, nor of the early years of Emperor Tiberius; no one seeks an exemplar beyond you, for it is you they wish to imitate. Your rule has been subjected to the test of the crucible—a test which it would have been difficult to resist, had your goodness been feigned for the moment, instead of its being (as it is) an innate quality of yours. . . . . The Roman people ran a great risk, uncertain whither your noble disposition would end. But the prayers of the people have been answered ere this. There is no danger, unless you should suddenly become forgetful of your own self. . . . . All your citizens today are compelled to make this confession—that they are happy; and this second confession—that nothing can be added to their complete happiness except the assurance that it may endure forever. Many causes urge them to this acknowledgment (the very last which man ever condescends to make)—their deep security, their prosperity, and their faith that the laws will be administered with absolute justice. There flits before our eyes a contented State, to whose complete freedom nothing is lacking except the liberty of its dying.

It would be beyond our purpose to quote more of Seneca. It will suffice to give references to an earlier and to a later work. For the former consult the *Ludus* (written in 54 A. D.), i, 1; iv, 1; xii, 2. For the latter, *Naturales quaestiones* (finished before 64 A. D.), vi, 8, 3; vii, 17, 2; 21, 3.

17. Suet., *Nero*, 10.
18. Suet., *op. cit.*, 19, with which cf. Petrarch, Vol. III, p. 273.
19. *Ibid.*, 22 (cf. Petrarch, *loc. cit.*).
20. *Ibid.*, 12 (cf. Petrarch, *loc. cit.*).
21. *Ibid.*, 22 (cf. Petrarch, *loc. cit.*).
22. It may, perhaps, prove interesting to the reader to see by what epithets Nero is referred to in the *Octavia*. From a cursory reading of the tragedy we glean the following: "vir crudelis" (Nutrix, 49); "capax scelerum" (Nutrix, 158); "immitis" (Nutrix, 182); "impius" (Chorus, 374); "dirus" (Chorus, 674); "coniunx scelestus" (Octavia, 230); "saevus" (Octavia, 667); "princeps nefandus" (Octavia, 232); "cruentus" (Chorus, 681); "ferus" (Chorus, 703); "dux saevus" (Octavia, 240); "impius" (Octavia, 242); "hostis deum hominumque" (Octavia, 245); "monstrum" (Chorus, 383); "natus crudelis" (Agrippina, 615),

"nefandus" (Agrippina, 655); "saevus" (Chorus 984); "tyrannus" (Octavia, 34, 115, 919); "ferus" (Agrippina, 621b, Octavia, 986).

23. Suet., *Nero*, 12.

24. Seneca, *De clementia*, i, 11, 1–3:

> While speaking of your clemency, no one will dare, in the same breath, to mention the name of the deified Augustus..... He displayed moderation and kindness, I grant you; but it was only after the sea of Actium had been dyed with Roman blood, after his own and his enemy's fleets had been destroyed off the coast of Sicily, after the slaughter and proscriptions at Perugia. As for me, I do not call exhausted cruelty mercy. This, O Caesar, this which you exhibit is true mercy—which conveys no idea of repentance for previous barbarity, which is immaculate, unstained by the blood of fellow-citizens..... You, O Caesar, have kept the State free from bloodshed, and your greatest boast is that throughout the length and breadth of your empire you have shed not a single drop of man's blood, which is all the more remarkable and amazing because no one has been intrusted with a sword at an earlier age than you.

In the *Octavia*, however, during a discussion between Seneca and Nero, in which the philosopher endeavors to destroy his pupil's belief in an emperor's right to rule by the sword, the author says of a ruler that to

> Give the world rest, his generation peace,
> This is the height of virtue, by this path

> May heaven be attained; this is the way
> The first Augustus, father of the land,
> Gained 'mid the stars a place and as a god
> Is worshiped now in temples (*Oct.*, 487-90).

And Nero, who could learn at least those sayings of his tutor that suited his fancy and served his purpose, thereupon replies in terms identical with those used by Seneca in *De clementia*, i, 11, 1-3. Granted that the *Octavia* was written by Seneca, this discussion gives a very human touch to the relationship between the subject and his sovereign.

25. Suet., *Nero*, 16 (cf. Petrarch, *loc. cit.*).

26. It is very probable that Petrarch received the first suggestion of the friendship between the philosopher and the apostle from the statement of St. Jerome, *De viris ill.*, 12 (*Seneca* [Teubner], III, p. 476):

> Lucius Annaeus Seneca of Cordova, disciple of Sotion the Stoic and uncle of the poet Lucan, was a man of the most temperate life. I should not place him in the catalogue of saints, were it not for those letters, which are read by so many, of Paul to Seneca and of Seneca to Paul. In these Seneca, though the tutor of Nero and the most powerful man of his age, says that he wished he held the same position among his fellow-men that Paul held among the Christians. He was killed by Nero two years before Peter and Paul received the crown of martyrs.

The correspondence referred to in the above is mentioned also by St. Augustine, *Ep.*, 153, 14 (Migne, Vol. XXXIII, col. 659). It consists of fourteen letters, which are given in the Teubner edition of Seneca, Vol. III, pp. 476-81. The wish said to have been expressed by Seneca is to be found in *Ep.*, xi, p. 479. The letter, however, which Petrarch seems to have had in mind—the one describing the persecution of the Christians in Rome—is *Ep.*, xii (*op. cit.*, p. 480), which I give in full, that Petrarch's state of mind may be the better appreciated.

Greetings, Paul most dear. Do you suppose that I am not saddened and afflicted by the fact that torture is so repeatedly inflicted upon the innocent believers of your faith? that the entire populace judges your sect so unfeeling and so perpetually under trial as to lay at your doors whatever wrong is done within the city? Let us bear it with equanimity, and let us persevere in the station which fortune has allotted, until happiness everlasting put an end to our suffering. Former ages were inflicted with Macedon, son of Philip, with Dareius and Dionysius. Our age, too, has had to endure a Caligula, who permitted himself the indulgence of every caprice. It is perfectly clear why the city of Rome has so often suffered the ravages of conflagration. But if humble men dared affirm the immediate cause, if it were permitted to speak with impunity in this abode of darkness, all men would indeed see all things. It is customary to burn at the stake both Christians and Jews on the charge of having plotted the burning of the city. As for that wretch, whoever he is, who derives pleasure from the butchering of men and who thus hypocritically veils his real intentions—that wretch awaits his hour. Even as all the best men are now offering their lives for the many, so will he some day be destroyed by fire in expiation of all these lives. One hundred and thirty-two mansions and four blocks of houses burned for six days, and on the seventh the flames were conquered. I trust, brother, that you are in good health. Written on the fifth day before the Kalends of April, in the consulship of Frugus and Bassus.

Petrarch elsewhere clearly states that he did not think Seneca a Christian, "tamen haud dubie paganum hominem," in spite of his having been placed by St. Jerome among the Christian writers, "inter scriptores sacros" (*Sen.*, XVI, 9, written in 1357).

The fourteen letters are today considered fictitious. Teuffel, par. 289 (and n. 9): "The estimation in which the writings of Seneca were held caused them to be frequently copied and abridged, but also produced at an early time such forgeries as the fictitious correspondence with the apostle Paul" (cf. also Wm. M. Ramsay, *St. Paul the Traveller and the Roman Citizen* [London, 1898], 4th ed., pp. 353-56).

IV. TO MARCUS VARRO
(*Fam.*, XXIV, 6)

Thy rare integrity, thine activity, and the great splendor of thy name urge me to love and in fact revere thee. There are some, indeed, whom we love even after their death, owing to the good and righteous deeds that live after them; men who mold our character by their teaching and comfort us by their example when the rest of mankind offends both our eyes and our nostrils; men who, though they have gone hence to the common abode of all (as Plautus says in the Casina¹), nevertheless continue to be of service to the living. Thou, however, art of no profit to us, or, at best, of only small profit. But the fault is not thine—it is due to Time, which destroys all things. All thy works are lost to us of today. And why not? 'Tis only of gold that the present age is desirous; and when, pray, is anyone a careful guardian of things despised?

Thou didst dedicate thyself to the pursuit of knowledge with incredible zeal and incomparable industry, and yet thou didst not for that reason abandon a life of action. Thou didst distinguish thyself in both directions, and deservedly didst become dear to those supremely eminent men, Pompey the Great and Julius Caesar. Thou didst serve as a soldier under the one; to the other thou didst address works worthy of admiration and full of the most varied learning*—a most remarkable fact when we consider that they were composed 'mid the widely conflicting duties of war and of peace. Thou art deserving of great praise not only for thy genius and for thy resolve to keep both mind and body in unremitting activity, but also for having had the power and the wish to be of service both to thy age and to all succeeding ages. But alas, thy works, conceived and elaborated with such great care, have not been deemed worthy of passing down to posterity through our hands. Our shameless indifference has undone all thine ardor. Never has there been a father ever so thrifty but that an extravagant son has been able to squander within a short time the accumulated savings of years.

But why should I now enumerate thy lost works? Each title is a stigma upon our name. It is better, therefore, to pass them over in silence; for probing only opens the wound afresh, and a sorrow once allayed is renewed by the memory of the loss incurred. But how incredible is the power of fame! The name lives on, even though the works be buried in oblivion. We have practically nothing of Varro[3], yet scholars unanimously agree that Varro was most learned.[4] Thy friend Marcus Cicero does not fear to make this unqualified assertion in those very books in which he maintains that nothing is to be asserted as positive. It is as if the splendor of thy name had dazzled him; as if, in speaking of thee, he had lost sight of the principles of his school.[5] Some there are who would accept this testimony of Cicero only within the narrow bounds of Latin literature, with whom therefore thou, O Varro, passest as the most learned of the Romans.[6] But there are some who include Greek literature as well, particularly Lactantius, a Roman most famous both for his eloquence and his piety, who does not hesitate to declare that no man has ever been more learned than Varro, not even among the Greeks.[7]

Among thy countless admirers, however, two stand out pre-eminently: one is he whom I have already mentioned, thy contemporary, thy fellow-citizen, and thy fellow-disciple, Cicero, with whom thou didst exchange numerous literary productions, thus devoting thy leisure moments to a useful occupation, in obedience to the precepts of Cato.[8] And if Cicero's works were more long-lived than thine, it must be accounted for by the charm of his style.[9] The second of thy pre-eminent admirers is a most holy man, and one endowed with a divine intellect, St. Augustine, African by birth, in speech Roman. Would that thou hadst been able to consult him when writing thy books on divine matters! Thou wouldst surely have become a very great theologian, seeing that thou hadst so accurately and so carefully laid down the principles of that theology with which thou wert acquainted. It has been written of thee that thou wert such an omnivorous reader as to cause wonder that thou couldst find any time for writing, and that thou wert so prolific a writer as to make it scarcely credible to us that anyone could even have read all that thou didst write.[10] And yet, that I may withhold nothing concerning the present condition of thy works, I shall say that there is not one extant, or at best they are only in a very fragmentary state. But I remember having seen some a long time ago,[11] and I am tortured by the memory of a sweetness tasted only with the tip of the tongue, as the saying goes. I am of the opinion that those very books on human and divine matters, which greatly increased the reputation of thy name, are still perchance in hiding somewhere, in search of which I have worn myself out these many years. For there is nothing in life more distressing and consuming than a constant and anxious hope ever unfulfilled.

But enough of this. Be of good cheer. Treasure the moral comfort deriving from thy uncommon labors, and grieve not that mortal things have perished. Even while writing thou must have known that thy work was destined to perish; for nothing immortal can be written by mortal man. Forsooth, what matters it whether our work perish immediately or after the lapse of a hundred thousand years, seeing that at some time it must necessarily die? There is, O Varro, a long line of illustrious men whose works were the result of an application equal to thine own, and who have not been a whit more fortunate than thou. And although not one of them was thy peer, yet thou shouldst follow their example and bear thy lot with greater equanimity. Let me enumerate some of this glorious company, for the mere utterance of illustrious names gives me pleasure." The following occur to me: Marcus Cato the censor, Publius Nigidius, Antonius Gnipho, Julius Hyginus, Ateius Capito, Gaius Bassus, Veratius Pontificalis, Octavianus Herennius, Cornelius Balbus, Masurius Sabinus, Servius Sulpitius, Cloacius Verus, Gaius Flaccus, Pompeius Festus, Cassius Hemina, Fabius Pictor, Statius Tullianus, and many others whom it would be tedious to enumerate, men once illustrious and now mere ashes blown hither and thither by every gust of wind. With the exception of the first two, their very names are scarcely known today. Pray greet them in my name, but alas, with thy lips. I do not send greetings to the Caesars Julius and Augustus and several others of that rank, even though they were devoted to letters and very learned, and though I know that thou wert very intimate with some of them. It will be better, I am sure, to leave the sending of such greetings to the emperors of our own age, provided they are not ashamed of their predecessors, whose care and courage built up an empire which they have overturned. Farewell forever, O illustrious one.

Written in the land of the living, in the capital of the world, Rome, which was thy fatherland and became mine, on the Kalends of November, in the year from the birth of Him whom I would thou hadst known, the thirteen hundred and fiftieth.

Notes on *Fam.*, XXIV, 6, to Varro

1. Plautus, *Casina, Prol.* 19, 20 (Leo).

2. The second part, at least, of the *Antiquitates*, treating of the "res divinae" and embracing books xxvi–xli, was addressed to Caesar as *Pontifex Maximus* (cf. below n. 7 and St. Aug., *De civ. dei*, VII, 35).

3. In 1354, the same year in which Petrarch received a copy of Homer from Niccolo Sigero, Boccaccio sent him a volume containing some works of Varro and of Cicero (cf. also *Sen.*, XVI, 1). Varro may have been represented by either the *De re rustica* or the *De lingua latina*, or by parts of both. In a letter of thanks for this favor, Petrarch draws a parallel between the two authors which is well worth quoting (*Fam.*, XVIII, 4):

No words that I might pen would prove equal to your kindness, and I feel sure that I should tire of expressing my appreciation much sooner than you of bestowing favors. I have received yet another book from you, containing some of the excellent and rare minor works of both Varro and Cicero. Nothing could have pleased nor delighted me more, for there was nothing that I more eagerly desired. What made the volume still more precious to me was that it was written in your hand.

In my opinion, this one fact adds you as a third to the company of those two great champions of the Latin tongue. Blush not at being classed with such illustrious men,

"Nor blush your lips to fill the rustic pipe,"

as the poet says.

You express admiration for those writers who flourished in the period of classical antiquity, the mother of all our studies—and rightly so, for it is characteristic of you to admire what the rabble despises and on the contrary to disdain what it so highly approves of. Yet the time will come when men will admire you perchance. Indeed, already has envy begun to signal you out. Men of superior intellect always meet with ungrateful contemporaries, and this ingratitude, as you are well aware, greatly depreciated for a time the works of the ancient authors. But fortunately succeeding generations, which at least in this respect were more just and less corrupt, gradually restored them to their place.

You showed, moreover, keen discrimination in gathering within the covers of one book two authors who, in their lifetime, were brought into such intimate relationship by their love of country, their period, their natural inclinations, and their thirst for knowledge. They loved each other and held each other in great esteem; many things they wrote to each other and of each other. They were two men with but one soul; they enjoyed the instructions of the same master, attended the same school, lived in the same State. And yet they did not attain the same degree of honor—'twas Cicero who soared higher. In short, they lived together in the best of harmony. And believe me, you could bring together few such men from all ages and all races. To follow common hearsay, Varro was the more learned, Cicero the more eloquent. However, if I should dare to speak my own say as to ultimate superiority, and if any god or man would constitute me judge in a question of such great importance, or rather would, without taking offense, deign to listen to a voluntary judgment on my part, I should speak freely and as my reason dictates. Both men are indeed great. My love and my intimate knowledge of one of them may, perhaps, deceive me. But the one whom I consider in every sense superior is—Cicero. Alas, what have I said? To what yawning precipice have I ventured? Oh well, the word has been spoken, the step taken. And may I be accused of great rashness rather than of small judgment. Farewell.

4. "Doctissimus" was as confirmed an epithet when speaking of Varro as "crafty" of Ulysses, "aged" of Nestor, "divus" of Augustus, etc. It is unnecessary to give here quotations from the Latin authors bearing out Petrarch's statement. Without seeking them at all, the following have been encountered in the preparation of these notes. St. Augustine, *De civ. dei*, III, 4: "vir doctissimus eorum Varro;" IV, 1: "vir doctissimus apud eos Varro et gravissimae auctoritatis;" IV, 31: "Dicit etiam idem auctor acutissimus atque doctissimus;" Seneca, *ad Helviam*, viii, 1; Apuleius, *Apol.*, 42.

5. The reference seems to be a direct one to Cicero's *Academica posteriora;* but the wording proves beyond doubt that our author is quoting instead from St. Augustine. Petrarch's words are (Vol. III, p. 275):

doctissimus Varro est, quod sine ulla dubitatione amicus tuus Marcus Cicero in iis ipsis libris in quibus nihil affirmandum disputat, affirmare non timuit, ut quodammodo luce tui nominis perstringente oculos, videatur interim dum de te loquitur suum principale propositum non vidisse.

St. Augustine says (*De civ. dei*, VI, 2):

in eis libris, id est Academicis, ubi cuncta dubitanda esse contendit, addidit "sine ulla dubitatione doctissimo." Profecto de hac re sic erat certus, ut auferret dubitationem, quam solet in omnibus adhibere, tamquam de hoc uno etiam pro Academicorum dubitatione disputaturus se Academicum fuisset [sic] oblitus.

The only variation between these two passages is that Petrarch has substituted for the simpler statement of St. Augustine the figure of the dazzling light.

Petrarch, however, did not have a first-hand acquaintance with the *Ac. posteriora*. In *Rer. mem.*, I, 2, p. 396, the chapter on Varro gives the entire substance of the present letter. According to Ancona-Bacci (Vol. I, p. 514), the *Liber rer. mem.* was composed earlier than

1350—the date of this letter to Varro—which therefore may have been modeled after the corresponding chapter of the *Rer. mem.*, in which *Ac. post.*, i, 3, 9 is cited in full. Hence it results that *Rer. mem.* I, 2 was based on St. Augustine, and *Fam.*, XXIV, 6, on *Rer. mem.*

6. St. Augustine distinctly says, *De civ. dei*, XIX, 22: "Varro doctissimus Romanorum;" and Quintilian, *Inst.*, x, 1, 95: "Terentius Varro, vir Romanorum eruditissimus."

7. Lactantius, *Divin. Inst.*, i, 6, 7: "M. Varro, quo nemo umquam doctior ne apud Graecos quidem vixit, in libris rerum divinarum quos ad C. Caesarem pontificem maximum scripsit. . . . ." (cf. Petrarch, Vol. III, p. 276).

8. *Catonis Disticha*, III, 5 (in *Poetae latini minores*, Vol. III):

Segnitiem fugito, quae vitae ignavia fertur;
Nam cum animus languet, consumit inertia corpus.

P. de Nolhac says (II, p. 110, n. 2) that he has not found in Petrarch a single reference to the *Catonis Disticha*, which were so widespread in the Middle Ages. The above, to be sure, is not actually cited by Petrarch, but it does seem to give the thought contained in "servata ex Catonis praecepto ratione otii" (III, p. 276).

9. St. Augustine, *De civ. dei*, VI, 2:

> And although Varro is less pleasing in his style, he is imbued with erudition and philosophy to such an extent that in every branch of those studies which we today call secular and which they were wont to call liberal, he imparts as much to him who is in pursuit of knowledge as Cicero delights him who is desirous of excelling in the choice of words.

This entire section (VI, 2) is a panegyric, and proves St. Augustine a great admirer of Varro. Quintilian, *Inst.*, x, 1, 95, is much briefer: "plus tamen scientiae conlaturus quam eloquentiae."

10. Petrarch (Vol. III, p. 276) quotes verbatim from St. Augustine, *De civ. dei*, VI, 2. The sense, at any rate, is perfectly clear in both passages, but seems to have escaped Fracassetti, who, after correctly rendering "tanto aver letto da far meraviglia che ti restasse tempo di scriver nulla," continues, "e scritto aver tanto che non s'intende come trovassi tempo per leggere alcuna cosa" (Vol. 5, p. 156).

We are reminded, too, of Cicero's similar boast regarding his own literary activity at Astura in 45 B. C., "Legere isti laeti qui me reprehendunt tam multa non possunt quam ego scripsi" (*ad Att.*, xii, 40, 2).

11. William Ramsay, in Smith's *Dict. of Grk. and Rom. Biogr.*, s. v. "Varro," says:

It has been concluded from some expressions in one of Petrarch's letters, expressions which appear under different forms in different editions, that the Antiquities were extant in his youth, and that he had actually seen them, although they had eluded his eager researches at a later period of life when he was more fully aware of their value. But the words of the poet, although to a certain extent ambiguous, certainly do not warrant the interpretation generally assigned to them, nor does there seem to be any good foundation for the story that these and other works of Varro were destroyed by the orders of Pope Gregory the Great, in order to conceal the plagiarism of St. Augustine.

And, to the opposite effect, J. A. Symonds, *The Revival of Learning*, (Scribner, 1900), p. 53, n. 3: "cf. his Epistle to Varro for an account of a MS of that author." P. de Nolhac is of the opinion that Petrarch's remembrances of the *Antiquitates* went through the same evolution as those of the *De gloria* (cf. the second letter to Cicero, n. 10).

12. With this sentiment compare the words of another enthusiastic humanist, John Addington Symonds, who writes (Preface, *op. cit.*, written in 1877): "To me it has been a labor of love to record even the bare names of those

Italian worthies who recovered for us in the fourteenth and fifteenth centuries 'the everlasting consolations' of the Greek and Latin classics."

V. TO QUINTILIAN
(*Fam.*, XXIV, 7)

I had formerly heard of thy name, and had read something of thine, wondering whence it was that thou hadst gained renown for keen insight. It is but recently that I have become acquainted with thy talents. Thy work entitled the *Institutes of Oratory* has come into my hands, but alas how mangled and mutilated! I recognized therein the hand of time—the destroyer of all things—and thought to myself, "O Destroyer, as usual thou dost guard nothing with sufficient care except that which it were a gain to lose. O slothful and haughty Age, is it thus that thou dost hand down to us men of genius, though thou dost bestow most tender care on the unworthy? O sterile-minded and wretched men of today, why do you devote yourselves to learning and writing so many things which it were better to leave unlearned, but neglect to preserve this work intact?"

However, this work caused me to estimate thee at thy true worth. As regards thee I had long been in error, and I rejoice that I have now been corrected. I saw the dismembered limbs of a beautiful body, and admiration mingled with grief seized me. Even at this moment, indeed, thy work may be resting intact in someone's library, and, what is worse, with one who perhaps has not the slightest idea of what a guest he is harboring unawares. Whosoever more fortunate than I will discover thee, may he be sure that he has gained a work of great value, one which, if he be at all wise, he will consider among his chief treasures.

In these books (whose number I am ignorant of, but which must doubtless have been many) thou hast had the daring to probe again a subject treated with consummate skill by Cicero himself when enriched by the experience of a lifetime. Thou hast accomplished the impossible. Thou didst follow in the footsteps of so great a man, and yet thou didst gain new glory, due not to the excellence of imitation but to the merits of the original doctrines propounded in thine own work. By Cicero, the orator was prepared for battle; by thee he is molded and fashioned, with the result that many things seem to have been either neglected or unheeded by Cicero. Thou gatherest all the details which escaped thy master's notice with such extreme care that (unless my judgment fail me) thou mayest be said to conquer him in diligence in just the degree that he conquers thee in eloquence. Cicero guides his orator through the laborious tasks of legal pleading to the topmost heights of oratory. He trains him for victory in the battles of the courtroom. Thou dost begin far earlier, and dost lead thy future orator through all the turns and pitfalls of the long journey from the cradle to the impregnable citadel of eloquence. The genius of Cicero is pleasing and delightful, and compels admiration. Nothing could be more useful to youthful aspirants. It enlightens those who are already far advanced, and points out to the strong the road to eminence. Thy painstaking earnestness is of assistance, especially to the weak, and, as though it were a most experienced nurse, offers to delicate youth the simpler intellectual nourishment.

But, lest the flattering remarks which I have been making cause thee to suspect my sincerity, permit me to say (in counterbalancing them) that thou shouldst have adopted a different style. Indeed, the truth of what Cicero says in his *Rhetorica* is clearly apparent in thy case, namely that it is of very little importance for the orator to discourse on the general, abstract theories of his profession, but that, on the contrary, it is of the very highest importance for him to speak from actual practice therein.[3] I do not deny thee experience, the second of these two qualities, as Cicero did to Hermagoras, of whom he was treating.[4] But I submit that thou didst possess the latter in only a moderate degree; the former, however, in such a remarkable degree that it seems now scarcely possible for the mind of man to add a single word.

I have compared this magnificent work of thine with that book which thou didst publish under the title *De causis*.[5] (And I should like to say in passing that this work has not been lost, that it might result the more clearly that our age is especially neglectful of only the highest and best things, and not so much so of the mediocre.) In such comparison it becomes plain to the minds of the discerning that thou hast performed the office of the whetstone rather than that of the knife,[6] and that thou hast had greater success in building up the orator than in causing him to excel in the courts. Pray do not receive these statements in bad part. For it is as true of thee as of others (and thou must be aware of the fact) that a man's intellectual powers are not equally suited for development in all directions, but that they will evince a special degree of qualification in one only. Thou wert a great man, I acknowledge it; but thy highest merit lay in thy ability to ground and to mold great men. If thou hadst had suitable material to hand, thou wouldst easily have produced a greater than thyself, O thou who didst so wisely develop the rare intellects intrusted to thy care!

There was, however, quite a jealous rivalry between thee and a certain other great man— I mean Annaeus Seneca. Your age, your profession, your nationality, even, should have been a common bond between you; but envy (that plague among equals) kept you apart. In this respect I think that thou, perhaps, didst exercise the greater self-restraint; for, whereas thou canst not get thyself to give him full praise, he speaks of thee most contemptuously. I myself should hesitate to be judged by an inferior. Yet, if I were constituted judge of such an important question, I should express this opinion. Seneca was a more copious and versatile writer, thou a keener; he employed a loftier style, thou a more cautious one. Furthermore, thou didst praise his genius and his zeal and his wide learning, but not his choice nor his taste. Thou dost add, in truth, that his style was corrupt, and vitiated by every fault.'⁷ He, on the other hand, numbers thee among those whose name is buried with them,⁸ although thy reputation is still great, and thou hadst been neither dead nor buried during his lifetime. For he passed away under Nero, whereas thou didst go from Spain to Rome under Galba, when both Seneca and Nero were no more. After many years thou didst assume charge of the grandnephews of Emperor Domitian by his express orders, and becamest sponsor for their moral and intellectual development.⁹ Thou didst fulfil thy trust, I believe, so far as lay in thy power and with hopeful prospects in both these directions; although, as Plutarch shortly afterward wrote to Trajan, the indiscretions of thy wards were made to detract from thine own fair name.¹⁰

I have nothing more to say. I ardently desire to find thee entire; and if thou art anywhere in such condition, pray do not hide from me any longer. Farewell.

Written in the land of the living, between the right slope of the Apennines and the right bank of the Arno, within the walls of my own city where I first became acquainted with thee, and on the very day of our becoming acquainted,¹¹ on the seventh of December, in the thirteen hundred and fiftieth year of Him whom thy master preferred to persecute rather than to profess.

Notes on *Fam.*, XXIV, 7, to Quintilian

1. Lapo di Castiglionchio gave Petrarch a copy of the *Institutes* in 1350. (For further details see n. 11.)

2. How very much like a prophecy this reads! But it was a most natural exclamation for the "first modern scholar," who stood at the threshold of the Renaissance, when so many of the classics had as yet to be discovered.

In a footnote of the Latin edition (Vol. III, p. 278), Fracassetti informs us that in one of the codices the following remark is added: "This turned out to be true, for the complete Quintilian was found at Constance." This refers to the discovery of a complete manuscript of Quintilian in 1416. The Florentine scholar Poggio Bracciolini, while attending the Council of Constance in the capacity of apostolic secretary, found this copy in an old tower of the monastery of St. Gall. It is, perhaps, the same as the one now preserved at Florence—the Codex Laurentianus.

The story of the discovery is well told in a letter by Poggio. This letter gives such a faithful picture of the enthusiasm of the humanists, and is of such great interest that, although rather a long letter, it has been thought best to give a translation of it here in full (from the Latin text of Jacques Lefant, *Poggiana*, Part IV, pp. 309-13):

POGGIO TO GUARINO OF VERONA

I am well aware that, in spite of your constant occupations, the receipt of my letters is always a source of great pleasure to you—so great is your politeness and singular kindness to all. I beg of you, however, to be particularly attentive in reading the present. I beseech you the more urgently, not because I am the possessor of that which even the most learned of men may be anxious to share, but rather out of respect due to that which I am going to tell you. I feel certain, since you are so pre-eminently learned, that the news will bring no slight enjoyment to you and to the other scholars.

For tell me, pray, what is there, or what can there be more pleasing, or agreeable, or acceptable to you and to others than the knowledge of those things by the study of which we become more learned and (what is of even greater moment) more discriminating in our likes and dislikes? Our great parent, nature, gave to the human race a reasoning mind, which we are to consult as our guide in the conduct of a good and happy life, than which nothing better could be imagined. I am not so sure but that, after all, by far the most extraordinary gift of nature is the power of speech, without which the reason and the intellect were of no avail.

Speech, in giving external expression to the workings of the mind, is the one faculty which distinguishes us from other creatures. We should therefore consider ourselves under deep obligation to all those who have developed the liberal arts, but under deepest obligation to those who, by their patient and unremitting study, have handed down to us the rules of oratory and the norms of correct speech. In short, although mankind is especially superior to all other living creatures through its use of speech, these scholars have striven that in just this respect men should excel themselves.

Many illustrious Roman authors devoted themselves to the study and to the development of the human speech, as you know. Chief and foremost among them was M. Fabius Quintilianus, who describes the method for the development of the perfect orator with such clearness, and with such characteristic carefulness that, in my opinion, he lacked nothing as regards either the broadest knowledge or the highest eloquence. Even if we possessed nothing of Cicero, the father of Roman eloquence, we should still attain to a perfect knowledge of correct speech with Quintilian alone as our guide.

Hitherto, however, among us (and by this I mean among us Italians) Quintilian was to be had only in such a mangled and mutilated state (the fault of the times, I think), that neither the figure nor the face of man was to be distinguished in him. [For the parts then missing see Sabbadini, *Scoperte*, p. 13, n. 64.] You yourself have seen him [*Aen.*, vi, 495-97]:

"His body gashed and torn,
His hands cut off, his comely face

Seamed o'er with wounds that mar its grace,
Ears lopped, and nostrils shorn."
—(Conington, ed. 1900, p. 195)

A grievous fact, indeed, and an insufferable, that in the foul mangling of so eloquent a man we should have inflicted such great loss upon the domain of oratory. But the greater was our grief and our vexation at the maiming of that man, the greater is our present cause for congratulation. Thanks to our searchings, we have restored Quintilian to his original dress and dignity, to his former appearance, and to a condition of sound health. [Andreolo Arese seems to have found a complete Quintilian in France as early as 1396. See Sabbadini, *op. cit.*, pp. 35, 36.]

Forsooth, if M. Tullius rejoices heartily in having secured the return of M. Marcellus from exile, and that too at a time when there were at Rome many other Marcelli who were just as good men, just as prominent and well known both at home and abroad, what are the learned men of today (and especially students of oratory) to do, seeing that this matchless glory of the Roman name (because of whose loss nothing was left except Cicero), and that this work, which but recently was so mangled and fragmentary, have been recalled not merely from exile but from utter destruction?

By Hercules, unless we had brought him aid in the nick of time, he would have died shortly. There is not the slightest doubt that that man, so brilliant, genteel, tasteful, refined, and pleasant could not longer have endured the filthiness of that dungeon, the squalor of that place, and the cruelty of those jailors. He was dejected and shabby in appearance, like unto those who have been condemned to death. His beard was unkept, and his hair matted with blood. [A quotation of *Aen.*, ii, 277.] His very features and dress cried out that he was sentenced to an undeserved death. He seemed to stretch out his hands to me, to implore the assistance of the Quirites to protect him against an unjust judge. He seemed to be making an accusation, in that he, who once had been the means of safety to so many with his resourceful eloquence, could now find not a single patron to take pity on his misfortune, not one who would consult for his safety or prevent his being led out to an unmerited end.

Often by mere chance, things come to pass which we do not dare to hope for, as Terence says [*Phormio*, 5, 1, vss. 30, 31]. And so Fortune (and not so much his as ours) would have it that, when we found ourselves at Constance with nothing to do, a sudden desire should seize us of visiting the place where Quintilian was imprisoned—the monastery of St. Gall, twenty miles away. And so several of us proceeded thither [among whom Bartolomeo da Montepulciano and Cencio Rustici: Sabbadini, *op. cit.*, p. 77] to relax our minds and at the same time to search through the volumes of which there was said to be a great number. There, among crowded stacks of books which it would take long to enumerate, we discovered a Quintilian, still safe and sound, but all moldy and covered with dust. For the books were not in the library, as their merit warranted, but in a most loathsome and dreary dungeon at the very foundations of one of the towers—a place into which not even those awaiting execution would be thrust.

I for one feel certain that if there were any today who would tear down these barbarian penitentiaries in which such men are held prisoners, and would submit them to a most careful search, as our predecessors did, they would meet with the same good fortune in the case of many authors whose loss we now mourn.

In addition to the Quintilian, we discovered the first three books and half the fourth book of the *Argonauticon* of C. Valerius Flaccus [books i–iv, 317: Sabbadini, *op. cit.*, p. 78]; and explanations or commentary on eight orations of Cicero by Q. Asconius Pedianus, a very eloquent man mentioned by Quintilian himself. All these I transcribed with my own hand, and somewhat hastily [the Quintilian in thirty-two days, Burckhardt, p. 189], for I was anxious to send them to Leonardo Bruni of Arezzo and to Niccoló of Florence [Niccoló Niccoli, for whom he was acting as agent].

You have now, my dearest Guarino, all that could be given to you, for the present, by one who is most devoted to you. I wish I could have sent to you the book as well. But I had to please our Leonardo first. Still, you now know where it is to be had, so that if you really want to have it (which I should judge to be as soon as possible), you can easily obtain it. Farewell.

At Constance, December 16, 1416.

The real date of the discovery is in June or July, 1416; cf. Sabbadini, *op. cit.*, p. 78.

3. Cic., *De inv.*, i, 6 *extr.*

4. Fracassetti translates this passage, Vol. 5, p. 160 (at bottom): "Non io peró, com'egli

ad Ermagora, a te vorrei dell'una o dell'altra cosa negare il vanto." From this rendering, one receives the impression that Cicero was equally ready to deny Hermagoras both theory and practice. Cicero, however, distinctly testifies to the theoretical ability of Hermagoras in the words "quod hic [i. e., H.] fecit," and just as distinctly affirms his lack of experience— "ex arte dicere, quod eum minime potuisse omnes videmus." The words of Petrarch now, therefore, become clear. He says (Vol. III, p. 279): "oratori minimum de arte loqui, multo maximum ex arte dicere. Non tamen ut ille [i. e., Cicero] Hermagorae de quo agebat, sic ego tibi horum alterum eripio."

5. This work has sometimes been wrongly identified with the *Dialogus de oratoribus*, which was not known until the fifteenth century. The *De causis* mentioned by Petrarch must be a reference to the collection of *Declamationes* which in the Middle Ages passed as the work of Quintilian (P. de Nolhac, II, pp. 84, n. 3, and 85; Teuffel, par. 325 and n. 11).

6. Horace, *Ars Poetica*, 304, 305.

7. These criticisms are to be found in Quintilian, book x. Since Petrarch uses almost the same words, and in fact quotes verbatim

in the last instance, the tenth book (or at least this portion of it) must have been part of the Quintilian given him by Lapo di Castiglionchio (see n. 11). Petrarch says (Vol. III, p. 280): "et tu [i. e., Quintilian] quidem ingenium eius et studium et doctrinam laudas [Quint., x, 1, 128], electionem ac iudicium non laudas [x, 1, 130]: stilum vero corruptum et omnibus vitiis fractum dicis [x, 1, 125]." (For the parts of the *Institutes* generally missing in the Middle Ages, see Sabbadini, *Scoperte*, p. 13, n. 64.)

8. Sen., *Contr.*, x, *praef.* 2: "Pertinere autem ad rem non puto . . . . quomodo L. Asprenas aut Quintilianus senex declamaverit: transeo istos quorum fama cum ipsis extincta est." This criticism, evidently, was not spoken by Seneca the philosopher, as Petrarch thought, but by the elder Seneca, the author of the *Controversiae* and *Suasoriae*. Petrarch has simply confused the two, not being aware of the existence of the latter. Furthermore, the elder Seneca died before or about the time that Quintilian was born. Hence the criticism could not have referred to the author of the *Institutes*, but, perhaps, to Quintilian's father (who is merely mentioned in Quint., ix, 3, 73), or to Sextus Nonius Quintilianus, consul in 8 A.D.

In either case the identity of this other Quintilian remains a doubtful one.

9. There is no question that Quintilian's pupils were the sons of Flavius Clemens and Domitilla the Younger—in other words, the grandsons of Emperor Domitian's sister, and hence his grandnephews. The Italian version wrongly gives (Vol. 5, p. 162): "i figli di sua sorella, nipoti suoi—the sons of his sister, his nephews." Petrarch's Latin reads (Vol. III, p. 280): "sororis Domitiani principis nepotum curam ipso mandante suscipiens." The confusion seems to arise from the double function of the Italian word "nipoti" for both "nephews" and "grandchildren."

10. Plutarch, *Moralia* (ed. Gregorius N. Bernardakis), Vol. VII, p. 183, "Institutio Traiani, Epistola ad Traianum," 11, 7-16:

I therefore congratulate you upon your merits, and myself upon my good fortune, provided that in the exercise of your power you exhibit the same justice and honesty which have earned it for you. Otherwise I am sure that you will be exposed to serious dangers, and that I shall be subjected to the criticism of my detractors. For Rome cannot tolerate worthless emperors, and men, in their gossiping, are wont to heap upon teachers the faults of their pupils. In consequence, Seneca is justly censured by those who detract from his Nero, Quintilian is justly charged with the rash acts of his wards, and

Socrates is justly accused of having been over-indulgent with his pupil.

Petrarch's words, "tuorum adolescentium temeritas in te refunditur" (Vol. III, p. 280), are directly quoted from the pseudo-Plutarch's "adolescentium suorum temeritas in Quintilianum refunditur." Cf. also Petrarch, *De rem.*, I, 81.

11. Fracassetti omits to translate this thought, though it seems to result clearly from Petrarch's words (Vol. III, p. 280): "Apud superos .... ubi primum mihi coeptus es nosci, eoque ipso tempore." In the Latin edition Fracassetti notes that in one of the codices in the Laurentian Library, Lapo di Castiglionchio entered the following comment on these words: "You speak truly, for it was I who presented you with that work while you were on your way to Rome—a work which, as you said, you had never seen before." The omission mentioned above seems, however, to have been a mere slip. For elsewhere, in speaking of the same occurrence, Fracassetti says (Vol. 2, p. 249): "a lui [Petrarca] Lapo fece la prima volta conoscere, e donó le Istituzioni di Quintiliano, per lo acquisto delle quali egli nel giorno stesso scrisse una lettera a Quintiliano medesimo."

VI. TO TITUS LIVY
(*Fam.*, XXIV, 8)

I should wish (if it were permitted from on high) either that I had been born in thine age or thou in ours; in the latter case our age itself, and in the former I personally should have been the better for it. I should surely have been one of those pilgrims who visited thee. For the sake of seeing thee I should have gone not merely to Rome, but indeed, from either Gaul or Spain I should have found my way to thee as far as India.[1] As it is, I must fain be content with seeing thee as reflected in thy works—not thy whole self, alas, but that portion of thee which has not yet perished, notwithstanding the sloth of our age. We know that thou didst write one hundred and forty-two books on Roman affairs. With what fervor, with what unflagging zeal must thou have labored; and of that entire number there are now extant scarcely thirty.[2]

Oh, what a wretched custom is this of wilfully deceiving ourselves! I have said "thirty," because it is common for all to say so. I find, however, that even from these few there is one lacking. They are twenty-nine in all, constituting three decades, the first, the third, and the fourth, the last of which has not the full number of books.³ It is over these small remains that I toil whenever I wish to forget these regions, these times, and these customs. Often I am filled with bitter indignation against the morals of today, when men value nothing except gold and silver, and desire nothing except sensual, physical pleasures. If these are to be considered the goal of mankind, then not only the dumb beasts of the field, but even insensible and inert matter has a richer, a higher goal than that proposed to itself by thinking man. But of this elsewhere.

It is now fitter that I should render thee thanks, for many reasons indeed, but for this in especial: that thou didst so frequently cause me to forget the present evils, and transfer me to happier times. As I read, I seem to be living in the midst of the Cornellii Scipiones Africani, of Laelius, Fabius Maximus, Metellus, Brutus and Decius, of Cato, Regulus, Cursor, Torquatus, Valerius Corvinus, Salinator, of Claudius, Marcellus, Nero, Aemilius, of Fulvius, Flaminius, Attilius, Quintius, Curius, Fabricius, and Camillus. It is with these men that I live at such times and not with the thievish company of today among whom I was born under an evil star. And Oh, if it were my happy lot to possess thee entire, from what other great names would I not seek solace for my wretched existence, and forgetfulness of this wicked age! Since I cannot find all these in what I now possess of thy work, I read of them here and there in other authors, and especially in that book where thou art to be found in thy entirety, but so briefly epitomized that, although nothing is lacking as far as the number of books is concerned, everything is lacking as regards the value of the contents themselves.[4]

Pray greet in my behalf thy predecessors Polybius and Quintus Claudius and Valerius Antias, and all those whose glory thine own greater light has dimmed; and of the later historians, give greeting to Pliny the Younger, of Verona, a neighbor of thine, and also to thy former rival Crispus Sallustius. Tell them that their ceaseless nightly vigils have been of no more avail, have had no happier lot, than thine.

Farewell forever, thou matchless historian!

Written in the land of the living, in that part of Italy and in that city in which I am now living and where thou wert once born and buried, in the vestibule of the Temple of Justina Virgo, and in view of thy very tombstone;[5] on the twenty-second of February, in the thirteen hundred and fiftieth year[6] from the birth of Him whom thou wouldst have seen, or of whose birth thou couldst have heard, hadst thou lived a little longer.

николая Notes on *Fam.*, XXIV, 8, to T. Livy

1. Petrarch briefly relates the same story in *Rer. mem.*, II, 2, "De Ingenio." He says, p. 411:

> In what rank, indeed, will Titus Livy be placed, whose great reputation for eloquence drew illustrious and admiring men from the remotest corners of the globe all the way to Rome? This is related by Pliny, and in later years it was repeated by St. Jerome in the beginning of his preface to the book of Genesis, placed thus at the beginning that no one might be excused for being ignorant of it. How great must have been the excellence of that work, when, over immense distances of land and sea, men rushed to the mistress of the world, to that city which held sway over conquered nations, not to accomplish any urgent business transaction, not because of a desire to see the city itself (and that, too, such as it must have been under Caesar Augustus), but that they might see and hear that single one of its inhabitants.

Pliny tells the story in *Ep.*, ii, 3, 8; but Pliny the Younger was an author unknown to Petrarch (P. de Nolhac, I, p. 129, n. 1, and p. 235, n. 3; Sabbadini, *Scoperte*, p. 26). The reference to St. Jerome is *Ep.*, 53, written to Paulinus *ca.* 394 A. D., which appears as the first of the *Praefationes* in the 1903 edition of the Vulgate,

p. xviii (by Valentinus Loch). Petrarch therefore must have had the letter of St. Jerome in mind, or before him. In his own letter to Livy, Petrarch mentions both Gaul and Spain. In Pliny there is mention of Cadiz only. Both Gaul and Spain, however, are mentioned by St. Jerome. Furthermore, the references to Livy's being the one great man in Rome at that time, and to the splendor of the city under Augustus, are both traceable to St. Jerome, who, therefore, must have been the source for both the passage in the *Rer. mem.*, and for that in this letter to Livy. The passage in St. Jerome reads as follows, Vol. XXII, col. 541 (ed. Migne):

> Ad T. Livium lacteo eloquentiae fonte manantem, de ultimis Hispaniae Galliarumque finibus quosdam venisse nobiles legimus; et quos ad contemplationem sui Roma non traxerat, unius hominis fama perduxit. Habuit illa aetas inauditum omnibus saeculis celebrandumque miraculum, ut urbem tantam ingressi, aliud extra urbem quaererent.

Finally, that this passage from St. Jerome was the source used by Petrarch is proved also by *Sen.*, XVI (XV), 7 (*Op.*, p. 958):

> St. Jerome records having read that certain prominent men undertook the long journey from the furthermost limits of Spain and the two Gauls to Rome merely to see Livy. Do you for a moment suppose that there was

insufficient cause, not merely for these few men, but indeed for the whole world to rush thither, that they might see the man with their own eyes and hear him with their own ears? I shall here omit styling him a pure fountain of eloquence, as St. Jerôme did (*Ep.*, 53), or an overflowing fountain of eloquence—an epithet which Valerius used in speaking of his Pompeius [Val. Max., ii, 6, 8. The *Pompeius* referred to is No. 20 in Smith's *Dict.* Fracassetti goes entirely astray in the translation of this passage, *Sen.*, 2, p. 503]. Still, how commendable a desire was it to see that man who, even if he had done nothing else in his life, or if he could have added not a single thought to his work, had already earned everlasting renown for completing unaided and in 142 books, that stupendous work containing the entire history of Rome from its very origins! Moreover, C. Caligula to the contrary notwithstanding (Suet., *Cal.*, 34), this work was written throughout in a divine style and with extreme care. It was a work approaching the miraculous. The life of a single man would scarcely suffice even to transcribe this work, much less to produce a similar one. How worthy a desire was it, then, to behold the head which had conceived so much, and the hand which had penned such noble words of such noble deeds! If T. Livy were alive today, I believe that not merely a few, but very many would set out on their pilgrimage to him. As for myself, if my health were sounder (as it was but recently), if it were as strong as my desires, and if the road were safe, I should not consider it irksome to seek him, not merely at Rome, but as far as India, setting out from this very city of Padua which gave him birth and where I have now been staying for many years.

The letter from which the above is quoted bears the date Padua, May 12, 1373.

2. The extent of Petrarch's acquaintance with Livy results even more clearly from a passage in another of his works. It is short enough to be quoted in full. In *Rer. mem.*, I, 2, "De studio et doctrina," Petrarch, after giving examples of native-born Romans, says, p. 397:

And now, in going beyond the walls of the city, we need not at once leave the confines of Italy. With what ardor must T. Livy of Padua have toiled, who, within the compass of 142 books, wrote a complete history of Rome from the founding of the city to the reign of Caesar Augustus, under whom he flourished? This was a work remarkable for its mere bulk; and it was a stupendous work particularly for this reason—that in composing it he did not write hurriedly, nor (as the saying goes) did he employ a confused and disordered style, as certain others do, who slap down in writing every word that happens to be on the tip of their tongue. On the contrary, the history of Livy is couched in sentences of such great majesty and in words of such dignity and propriety that it is practically a textbook for choice and elegant diction.

But alas! Oh, lasting shame of our age! Scarcely a small portion of this great and splendid work survives. Of the 14 decades into which it was subdivided—either by the author himself, or (as I think more likely) by the indolent readers of later generations—there are extant but three! These are the first, the third, and the fourth. At the urgent request of King Robert of Sicily (of sacred memory), I myself have searched most diligently for the second decade, but up to this moment I have searched in vain. I pray I may be provèd to be a false prophet. But unless customs change, I fear lest within a short time that very fate overtake Livy which formerly it was the intention of Gaius Caligula, most hateful of tyrants, to bring upon him. For we read in Suetonius Tranquillus that Caligula had been on the point of removing from all libraries the history of T. Livy and the works and busts of the poet Vergil. I fear then, that, although an emperor's cruelty proved insufficient, our own regardless inactivity may gradually succeed in casting the veil of oblivion over the resplendent genius of this man.

The reference to Suetonius is *Cal.*, 34, which Petrarch quotes almost verbatim, his words being: "quod T. Livii historiam, et Virgilii poetae libros et imagines, parum abfuit, quin ab omnibus bibliothecis amoveret."

3. We are indebted to the excellent study of P. de Nolhac so often cited (*Pétrarque et l'humanisme*) for exact information on this point. The book missing from the manuscript of Livy which Petrarch possessed was book xxxiii. On fol. 317, in commenting on the words "Cynoscephalas, ubi debellatum erat cum Philippo" (Livy, xxxvi, 8), Petrarch wrote in the margin,

"Sed quando hoc fuerat deficit sine dubio, et ut puto unus liber." Even book xl was not complete, although Petrarch may not have been aware of the fact, since he does not complain thereof. His manuscript ended with the words, "conciliabulaque edixerunt" (chap. 37) which seemed to close the book in a manner making complete sense (P. de Nolhac, II, p. 16). Baeumker (*Quibus antiquis auctoribus Petrarca in conscribendis rerum memorabilium libris usus sit*, p. 14), went so far as to say (in 1882) that Petrarch did not have books xxxi-xxxv. It is now certain that Petrarch possessed the first and the third decades entire, and books xxxi, xxxii, and xxxiv to xl, the last of which ended with chap. 37—in all nearly twenty-nine books.

4. Petrarch here refers to the epitome of Florus. The Codex in Petrarch's possession contained the works of several historians—Dictys, Florus, Livy, etc. (see P. de Nolhac, II, p. 15), and had been bought by Petrarch at Avignon in 1351, after the death of Soranzio (or Soranzo) Raimondo, to whom it had probably belonged (*ibid.*, p. 21). The date of the purchase almost compels us to adopt 1351 as the date of this letter (see n. 6).

5. Between the years 1335 and 1344 there was found in the monastery of Santa Giustina of Padua a sepulchral inscription bearing the name of T. Livius. Without troubling themselves with further investigations, the Benedictine monks who had made the discovery jumped to the conclusion that the stone was that which had been erected over the dead Roman historian. They consequently placed it in the vestibule of their church, and over it placed a likeness of the historian. Petrarch was stopping at the cloister opposite the church of Santa Giustina; thus the phrase employed at the close of the letter is clear.

In 1413 a leaden casket came to light in the same place. Inasmuch as the monks had learned from those of the previous generation that Livy had been buried there, they concluded (again without warrant) that the casket must contain the remains of Livy, although (as Polentonus says) there were not lacking, even at that time, those who denied the fact. For a description of the great ado caused by this supposed discovery, read the letter by Sicco Polentonus, quoted in the introductory note to *Corpus inscriptionum latinarum*, V, 2865. The inscription itself was believed to be that of Livy until the middle of the seventeenth century (P. de Nolhac, II, p. 12, n. 3).

6. P. de Nolhac (II, p. 12, n. 3) says that the Paris manuscript bears the date 1351 (cf. n. 4 above).

VII. TO ASINIUS POLLIO
(*Fam.*, XXIV, 9)

Long ago the thought entered my mind of addressing letters of familiar intercourse to certain far-off masters of eloquence, embracing in the number those who had been the rare ornaments of the Latin tongue. I should not wish, therefore, to pass thy name over in silence, the more so that, according to the testimony of great writers, thy fame was second to none. Since, however, thy reputation has come down to us stripped almost bare of facts, it must be substantiated by the writings of others rather than of thyself, a fact which I deservedly number among the shameful losses of our age. I shall have, therefore, but little to say to thee.

I congratulate thee in that thou didst enjoy the honors of a consulship as well as those of a triumph;[1] I congratulate thee for the praises bestowed upon thy lofty intellect and polished eloquence, and for thy many other endowments of body and mind and fortune.[2] I give thee special congratulations, however, for having lived under the best of princes, who cherished most dearly both letters and virtues, and who was a competent judge of thy deeds. O happy thou, who didst fill the just measure of thy life while Augustus was still reigning, bringing an illustrious life to a peaceful close at thy Tusculan villa and in the eightieth year of thine age.[3] Thou didst escape the bloody hands of Tiberius, into which the orator Asinius Gallus fell, thy ill-fated offspring who, as we read, was killed by him with dreadful suffering.[4] Fortunate indeed was it that a timely death overtook thee, seeing toward what great misery thy destiny was already beginning to urge thee. Death saved thine eyes from witnessing such a sad spectacle at least. Only a few years more and, to thy great sorrow, thou wouldst have shared the fate of thy son, or wouldst have been compelled to look on.[5] His death must have diminished thy happiness in no slight degree—if it be true (as some thinkers claim) that the dead are affected by the lot of the living.

The laws of true friendship forbid me to conceal or pass over a certain thing in silence—for friendship binds me to the names and ashes of the illustrious dead of every age no less effectually than if they were alive. The thing, therefore, which greatly distressed me in thee was, that thou didst resolve to be such a very bitter and severe critic (not to say censurer) of Marcus Tullius.⁶ In all justice thou shouldst have been the first to praise and exalt his name in thy writings. If thy defense is that thou hadst a right to freedom of thought, I shall answer that I do not deny thee such freedom, even though I do not agree with thy conclusions. I maintain, however, that thou shouldst have made more sparing use of thy freedom. Such counsel comes too late now, I know. Yet thou canst easily obtain indulgence from others' since thou didst so often exercise the same freedom against him who was then ruling the universe.⁸

It is rather difficult, I grant thee, for fortune's favorite to curb the mind and the tongue. The seriousness of purpose consonant with thy great age and learning compels me to exact from thee careful consideration in all matters. Furthermore, it obliges me to censure thee for thy actions more severely than I should either thy son, who held the same opinions as thou because he followed in thy footsteps,⁹ or Calvus and others of the same party.¹⁰

I am not so forgetful of myself as to deny thee the exercise of the same privilege in the case of a contemporary (whom thou couldst both see and know) that I have enjoyed, after so many centuries, in the case of a man of such reputation and so far removed from me in time. No one is perfect. Who, then, shall forbid thee, a man of such eminence, to call attention to anything reprehensible in the ways of thy neighbor, when even I who am so far removed have found things to criticise in his writings? But the moment thou dost attack his reputation for eloquence, the moment thou dost endeavor to wrest from him his supremacy in the field of oratory—a supremacy bestowed upon him from heaven and granted to him without dispute and by the common consent of nearly the entire world—that moment see to it that thou be not inflicting too palpable an injury.

Beware, and with thee let Calvus beware, that you do not enter upon an ill-matched struggle against Cicero for the palm in oratory. It is a very easy task for us to watch the contest as spectators. But the crown of victory has long since been awarded." You have been conquered. Vain are your struggles and obstructions! The ruffling of your own pride prevents you from seeing the truth. In my opinion you would have been great men, had you been able to acknowledge a greater than yourselves. But man, in his pride, is raised by false opinions to higher levels than those to which he rightfully belongs; and from this high station truth then causes him to sink to a lower level than he might justly have deserved. Many have lost their own reward of glory in hungering after that of others.

It was envy, perchance, that prompted your actions, for those of your companions who envied Cicero were as numerous as those who were blinded by their pride. If so, again am I more vexed at thee than at Calvus, for the latter had some cause, in fact had good cause, not merely for envying Cicero but for hating him." I know of not the slightest cause for hatred in thy case. And therefore it seems all the more a pity to me that envy, which is wont to creep along the ground, should have seized upon so lofty an intellect as was thine.

Farewell forever. Of the Greek orators, give greetings to Isocrates, Demosthenes, and Aeschines; of the Romans, to Crassus and Antonius, and indeed to Corvinus Messala and Hortensius, provided that the former of these last two, now that he is rid of the encumbrances of the flesh, has regained the memory which he lost two years before departing hence,"³ and that the latter has not lost his.

In a suburb of Milan, on the first of August of this last age the thirteen hundred and fifty-third year.

NOTES ON *Fam.*, XXIV, 9, TO ASINIUS POLLIO

1. Suet., *Rel.* (Teubner), p. 289, ll. 34 f.: "Asinius Pollio orator et consularis, qui de Dalmatis triumphaverat, in villa Tusculana anno octogesimo aetatis suae moritur" (St. Jerome, *Chron.*, a. Abr., 2020, in Migne, Vol. XXVII, col. 441, and Reiff., p. 82).

2. Some examples of praises bestowed upon Pollio are: Catullus, *Carm.*, xii, 9: Horace, *Carm.*, ii, 1, 13: Quintilian, x, 2, 25; xii, 10, 11; x, 1, 113 has praise mingled with censure:

Asinius Pollio possesses a well-developed faculty of invention, and great accuracy not only of language (which to some, indeed, appears too accurate), but also of method and of spirit. But he is so far from possessing the brilliant and pleasing style of Cicero that he might seem to belong to the preceding century.

3. See n. 1 above.

4. See Smith's *Dict:*

Tiberius hated him, partly on account of his freedom in expressing his opinion, but more especially because Asinius Gallus had married Vipsania, the former wife of Tiberius. At last the emperor resolved upon getting rid of him. In A.D. 30 he invited him to his table at Capreae, and at the same time got the senate to sentence him to death. But Tiberius saved his life, only for the purpose of inflicting upon him severer cruelties than death alone. He kept him imprisoned for three years, and on the most scanty supply of food. After the lapse of three years, he died in his dungeon of starvation, but whether it was compulsory or voluntary is unknown.

The last comment is from Tac., *Ann.*, vi, 23. The text which Petrarch must have had before him (and from which he practically quotes), is Suet., *Rel.* (Teubner), p. 290, ll. 27 f.: "C. Asinius Gallus Asinii Pollionis filius, cuius etiam Virgilius meminit [in *Ecl.*, 4], diris a Tiberio suppliciis necatur." Petrarch's words are (Vol. III, p. 283): "quem diris ab illo suppliciis enecatum legimus" (St. Jerome, in Migne, Vol. XXVII, col. 443, and Reiff., p. 86).

5. C. Asinius Pollio died in 5 A. D.; his son Gallus died in 33 A. D. (See preceding note.)

6. Quintilian, xii, 1, 22:

I pass over those who do not give Cicero and Demosthenes due credit even in oratory. To be sure, Cicero himself does not judge Demosthenes absolutely perfect, saying that now and then the latter becomes drowsy. Cicero is similarly judged by both Brutus and Calvus, who criticize the structure of his periods to his own face; and by the Asinii, father and son, who in many places attack the faults of his language even with bitterness.

Pollio's hostility to Cicero is mentioned also in Sen., *Suas.*, vi, 14; 24; 27. But Cicero was not the only author who displeased the taste of Pollio; among others were Livy (Quint., i, 5, 56; viii, 1, 3), Sallust (Suet., *Gramm.*, 10), and Caesar (see n. 8).

7. Sen., *Contr.*, iv, *praef.* 3:

(Pollio) was somewhat more ornate when declaiming than when pleading a case, ... and his judgment was so deficient that in many instances he himself stood in need of that indulgence which it was scarcely possible for others to obtain from him.

8. Petrarch's words are (Vol. III, p. 284): "adversus ipsum mundi Dominum." It will be noticed that Fracassetti prints the word "Dominum" with a capital letter, thus making the phrase equivalent to the word "God." In fact he translates the passage "contro lo stesso Signore della terra" (Vol. 5. p. 167), which conveys the same thought. Aside from the fact that Pollio died in A. D. 5, when it was quite too early to speak of Christianity at Rome, we believe that the line in Petrarch can easily be interpreted otherwise. The key is furnished by Suet., *Julius*, 56:

Asinius Pollio thinks that Caesar's books (on the Gallic War) were written with small accuracy and with but little regard for the truth. For, he says, Caesar was too ready to believe the accounts of deeds performed by others, and published in incorrect form even his own deeds, either purposely or because they had slipped his memory. Pollio, therefore, was of the opinion that Caesar would have rewritten or corrected his work.

And thus it clearly results that it is Caesar who is meant by "ipsum mundi Dominum."

9. There is a passage in Gellius written so very much after the heart and spirit of Petrarch, that the temptation to give it here has been too strong to resist. It is *Noc. Att.*, xvii, 1, 1:

Just as there have been in this world some monsters of men, who have scattered broadcast unholy and lying doctrines concerning the immortal gods, so have there been men so monstrous and so destitute of reason as to have had the presumption to write of Cicero that his language was by no means pure, and that it gave evidence of a faulty and inconsiderate choice of words. Among these detractors are Asinius Gallus and Largus Licinius, whose book is even yet current under the unspeakable title of *Ciceromastix*.

These words are such as might have been spoken by the venerable old gentleman of *Fam.*, XXIV, 2. (See the first letter to Cicero, n. 1.)

10. Sen., *Contr.*, vii, 4, 6: "Calvus who for a long time carried on a very unequal struggle against Cicero for supremacy in oratory."

11. Petrarch enlarges upon this point in *Rer. mem.*, II, 2, "De ingenio," p. 412:

It does not seem fitting to omit mention of Asinius Pollio, who, as Seneca has established and as is apparent to all, must be thought to hold the second place of honor between those two very eloquent Romans, M. Tullius and T. Livy [Sen., *Ep.*, 100, 9]. Seneca is an authority by no means to be despised. Thus far in the present chapter (*Rer. mem., loc. cit.*) I have written of six eloquent men. Seneca chooses none of these except Tullius, and maintains that there are three men foremost in eloquence —three whom in a certain letter of his he seems to prefer to all others. The second place among these he assigns to Pollio, whose style he pronounces different from that of Cicero, and (to use his own words) 'uneven and jolting and one that breaks off when you least expect it' [*Ep.*, 100, 7]. Although no specimens of his eloquence have as yet fallen into my hands, and although his name has already become famous and has already spread abroad unaided, still it did not appear just to me (when undertaking to write on the subject of eloquence) to pass his name in silence—the more so that I had already spoken of others inferior to him. And so it has pleased me to place him after Caesar Augustus, under whom he flourished. I shall add this only: that many sang the praises of Pollio; but that his name was especially honored by the Muse of Mantua. But I must now retrace my steps somewhat.

12. This is making it unnecessarily strong. Cicero's statements are more guarded, and

his criticisms are milder, than one would be led to suppose from the language of Petrarch. In the *Brutus*, where Cicero speaks of Calvus at great length, his language is reserved. In sec. 279 he says:

"I must first, however, do justice to the memory of two promising youths, who, if they had lived to a riper age, would have acquired the highest reputation for their eloquence." [In 280:] "You mean, I suppose," said Brutus, "Gaius Curio and Gaius Licinius Calvus." "The very same," replied I. . . . . [283:] But let us return to Calvus, whom we have just mentioned, an orator who had received more literary improvements than Curio, and had a more accurate and delicate manner of speaking, which he conducted with great taste and elegance; but (by being too minute and nice a critic upon himself) while he was laboring to correct and refine his language, he suffered all the force and spirit of it to evaporate. In short, it was so exquisitely polished, as to charm the eye of every skilful observer; but it was little noticed by the common people in a crowded forum, which is the proper theater of eloquence. (Translation of E. Jones, in the volume translated and edited by J. S. Watson.)

It must be noticed, however, that these passages were written after the death of Calvus; but we are compelled to judge from these, since none of the correspondence carried on between Cicero and Calvus on the subject of eloquence is now extant (cf. Cic., *ad Fam.*, XV, 21, 4, with which, however, Petrarch was unacquainted).

13. Pliny, *N. H.*, vii, 24, and St. Jerome, *Chron., a. Abr.*, 2027 (Migne, Vol. XXVII, coll. 441, 442, and Reiff., p. 83). From the similarity of expressions, it again results that St. Jerome was the direct source; for in Pliny there is no word alluding to the period of two years.

VIII. TO HORATIUS FLACCUS[1]
(*Fam.*, XXIV, 10)

O thou whom the Italian world hails as prince of the lyric song, to whom the Lesbian muse entrusted her lyre with its harmonious strings; O thou whom the Tyrrhenian Sea stole from the Adriatic, and Etruria from Apulia, and whom the Tiber claimed as its own, heeding not the cries of the Aufidus, nor spurning thy obscure and humble origin; sweet is it now to follow thee through secluded woodlands, to gaze upon the spring water bubbling up in the dimly lighted dales, to admire the purple hills and the verdant meadows, the cool lakes and the dewy grottos.[2]

It is sweet to go with thee, whether thou dost propitiate Faunus with his roaming flocks; or eagerly hasten to visit the impetuous and fiery Bromius; or perform the secret rites of the golden goddess related to the ivy-crowned Bacchus; or sing of Venus ever in need of both. 'Tis a joy to accompany thee when thou singest of the playful Nymphs and nimble Satyrs and of the Graces with their rosy, naked bodies;

or when thou dost sing the name and labors of the indomitable Hercules; or of the helmeted Mars, another offspring of incestuous Jove. 'Tis joyful to hear thee sing of the Aegis of Minerva, spreading terror far and wide with its Gorgon-head; or of the children of Leda, who sink beneath the waves and are the kind, protecting constellation of mariners; or of Mercury, the illustrious inventor of the lyre. How pleasing is it, when thou dost strike the praises of golden-haired Apollo, and dost bathe his glorious locks in the waters of the Xanthus; to hearken when thou dost extol his sister, distinguished by the quiver and striking terror to the hearts of the forest denizens, and when thou dost disclose the sacred dances of the Pierides.[3]

Thou dost chisel out the characters of the ancient heroes as though in material more lasting than marble. If thou but befriendest one, thou dost pen in his behalf fresh words of everlasting and enduring praise, such as time cannot erase. The spiritual spark of poets is of itself sufficient, when kindled by favorable impulses, to create undying pictures of men. It is due to these pen pictures that we see, as though yet alive, those demigods Drusus and

Scipio and the rest through whose agency far-renowned Rome imposed her yoke upon subjugated races. Among these heroes, like a sun gleaming with living light, there shines forth pre-eminently the race of the Caesars.[4]

Be thou my leader, for I am eager to hear thee sing these strains. Take me whither thou wilt. Lead me over the broad expanse of the sea dotted with sails; to the cloud-encompassed peaks of mountains. Take me from the channel of the flowing Tiber to where the Anio with its banks cuts its way through the fields—a region pleasing to thee formerly, when thou wert still of the living, and where I, musing, am weaving this chaplet for thee, O Flaccus, our glory. Lead me whither thou wilt: through forbidding forest darknesses, to the cold Algidus, to the warm waters of Baiae, the Sabine Lake, the fields strewn with flowers, and to Soracte's peak white with snows. Bear me with thee to Brundisium by the devious by-paths. I shall weary not; I shall gladly guide my slow footsteps in the company of such bards. Neither time nor tide will swerve me from my purpose. I shall march with equal vigor, if mother Earth be great with crops yet unharvested, or the dew be dried by the scorching rays of the sun, or the branches bend beneath their weight of fruit, or the earth be stiff and slow with cold. Under thy leadership I shall visit the shores of the Cyclades, the roaring waves of Thracian Bosporus, the lonely deserts of torrid Lybia, and the cold, stormy regions of far-off Caucasus.[5]

Wherever thou goest, whatever thou doest, pleases me. I am pleased when thou dost so carefully rouse thy faithful friends by giving virtue its due reward; when thou rendest vice with gnashing teeth, and when, smiling, thou dost artfully peck at folly. I am pleased when, singing sweetly, thou fillest thy song with tender words of love; when with sharp and vigorous pen thou upbraidest the riotous living of the old wanton; or when thou dost arraign the guilty city and dost accurse the drawn swords and savage frenzy of the Quirites. I rejoice when Maecenas is the burden of thy song—throughout thy work the first and last; when thou dost criticise the poets of the older school and dost disdain to tread in their footsteps; when thou pourest into the ears of magnanimous Caesar praises of his newly won honors. I am glad when, in one of thy poems, thou explainest to Florus thy reasons for declining to write any more satires or lyrics; when thou describest to Fuscus the joys of a country life and the evils of a turbulent city, and explainest to him why the warlike steed is the servant of man; glad, when thou teachest Crispus the true use of wealth. I am pleased when thou dost tear Vergil away from his unending grief and gently dost urge him to enjoy some relaxation and a few moments of pleasure at the coming of spring; when thou admonishest Hirpinus of the flight of time. I am pleased when thou remindest Torquatus and, in a similar ode, Postumus of the fleeting days and nights; when thou writest of old age stealthily creeping upon us all with noiseless tread, of the shortness of life which is gone even as we write, or of death which hastens after us with flying feet.[6]

Who would not enraptured listen when thou assignest Augustus (though still alive) to a place among the stars? or when, in accoutering Mars, thou declarest the inadequacy of iron and hast recourse to adamant? or when, as a conqueror, thou drivest along the Sacred Way and Hill, dragging bands of foreign princes bound to the triumphal chariots with fetters of gold, a victorious pomp which, feared and detested by a certain proud queen, caused her to welcome the inexorable sting of the asp? Who would not lend thee a willing ear, when thou recountest how the laws of hospitality were dishonored by the treacherous shepherd of Phrygia, and how from the quieted waves there came to Paris the threatening prophecy of Nereus? or how Danae is deceived by the shower of gold? or how the royal maiden, in spite of her grievous laments, is borne away on the back of the horned adulterer?'

Whether happy or alarmed, whether sad or angered, under any and all conditions thou dost give pleasure: either when thou frettest the anxious lover with manifold suspicions; or hurlest just imprecations on the snake-haired, poisonous hags and on the vulgar herd; when, free from cares, thou singest of Lalage; or when alone and with unruffled brow thou dost put to flight that desperate wolf; or when thou escapest the fall of the ill-omened tree, and the waves which had been lashed to fury by Aeolian winds.⁸

When I saw thee reclining upon the fresh turf, hearkening to the bubbling of the springs and to the songs of the birds, when I saw thee plucking the flowerets from the matted field, weaving the vinesprigs with the pliant osiers, touching the lyre with gentle fingers, changing the measures with splendid mastery, and soothing heaven itself with thy varied song—when I saw all this my eager mind suddenly became the prey of a noble desire, which spared me not till I had followed thee through all the recesses of the heaving sea, over cliffs and crags, 'mid the perils of sea and land. On the remotest confines of India I saw arise the gleaming steeds of the sun, and then did I behold them sink in the Western Ocean. In thy company I have roamed across the regions of the north wind and across the regions of the south wind. And now, whether thou leadest me to the Islands of the Blessed, or draggest me to wave-resounding Antium, or takest me to the citadels of Romulus, I shall follow thee with most eager mind, so happily am I drawn captive by the chords of thy lyre, so soothing is to me the bitter sweetness of thy pen.

Notes on *Fam.*, XXIV, 10, to Horatius Flaccus

1. This letter (as also the following one to Vergil) is written in verse, and is translated into verse by Fracassetti, who assigns to it the date 1337 or 1350. The chances are in favor of the later date; for Petrarch himself says (in the prefatory letter to Socrates, Vol. I, p. 25) that the letter he addressed to Cicero (*Fam.*, XXIV, 3, dated 1345) served as a precedent for the other letters to the classical authors. The letters to Horace and to Vergil really belong to the *Epistolae Poeticae*, the collection of which was dedicated to Barbato da Sulmona (*Fam.*, *praefatio*, I, pp. 15, 16, and *Fam.*, XXII, 3). Their presence here, then, must be due to the subject-matter.

A mere glance at the letter will reveal to the reader Petrarch's intimate knowledge of the complete works of Horace. Fracassetti says in this regard (Vol. 5, p. 177) that he did not trace the many allusions to their sources, because such labor would have proved utterly useless to one already acquainted with the works of

Horace, and would have been of very doubtful assistance to one who did not possess such knowledge. The nature of this study, however, demands the presence of the following notes. They will not be read, of course. They are given merely for the sake of reference and of completeness.

One word more. The allusions are so numerous that it has been thought best to give at the end of each paragraph the references to all the allusions contained therein. To facilitate identification, each reference is introduced by a caption of one or more words.

2. "secluded woodlands," *Carm.*, i, 17, 17; *Epod.*, ii, 11.

3. "Faunus," *Carm.*, i, 17; iii, 18; "Bromius," *ibid.*, ii, 19; iii, 25; "secret rites," *ibid.*, iii, 2; "ivy-crowned," *ibid.*, iii, 25, 20; iv, 8, 33; "in need of both," *ibid.*, i, 18, 6; 32, 9; iii, 21, 21; cf. Terence, *Eun.*, iv, 5, 6; "Nymphs," *Carm.*, i, 4; "Satyrs," *ibid.*, i, 1, 31; "naked bodies," *ibid.*, iii, 19, 17; iv, 7, 6; "Hercules," *ibid.*, i, 12, 25; iv, 5, 36; 8, 30; "Mars," *ibid.*, i, 2, 36; "Aegis," *ibid.*, i, 15, 11; iii, 4, 57; "Leda," *ibid.*, i, 12, 25; "constellation," *ibid.*, i, 12, 27, 28; iii, 29, 64; iv, 8, 31; "lyre," *ibid.*, i, 10, 6; "Xanthus," *ibid.*,

iv, 6, 26; "quiver," *ibid.*, iii, 4, 72; "terror," *ibid.*, i, 12, 22.

4. "Drusus," *Carm.*, iv, 4, 18; 14, 10; "Scipio," *Sat.*, ii, 1, 17 and 72; "shines forth," *Carm.*, i, 12, 46-48.

5. "glory," *Carm.*, i, 1, 2; "Algidus," *ibid.*, i, 21, 6; "warm waters," *Epist.*, i, 15, 5; "Sabine lake," *Carm.*, iv, 1, 19; "Soracte," *ibid.*, i, 9, 1 and 2; "Brundisium," *Sat.*, i, 5; "slow with cold," cf. *Carm.*, iii, 23, 5-8; iv, 7, 9-12; "Cyclades," *Carm.*, i, 14, 20; iii, 28, 14; "Bosporus," *ibid.*, ii, 20, 14; iii, 4, 30; "Lybia," *ibid.*, i, 22, 5 and 16; ii, 6, 3 and 4; "Caucasus," *ibid.*, i, 22, 7; *Epod.*, i, 12.

6. "wanton," *Carm.*, i, 25; iii, 15; iv, 13; "drawn swords," *Epod.*, 7 and 16; "school," *Sat.*, i, 4 and 10; "footsteps," *Epist.*, i, 19, 21-25; cf. *Carm.*, iii, 30, 13; "honors," *Carm.*, iii, 25, 7, 8; "Florus," *Epist.*, ii, 2; "Fuscus," *Epist.*, i, 10; "steed," *Epist.*, i, 10, 34-41; "Crispus," *Carm.*, ii, 2; "Vergil," *ibid.*, i, 24; "pleasure," *ibid.*, iv, 12; "Hirpinus," *ibid.*, ii, 11; "Torquatus," *ibid.*, iv, 7; "Postumus," *ibid.*, ii, 14; "fleeting days," *ibid.*, iv, 13, 16; cf. iii, 28, 6; "shortness of life," *ibid.*, iv, 13, 22; *Sat.*, ii, 6, 97; *Epist.*, ii, 1, 144; "as we

write," *Carm.*, i, 11, 7; "flying feet," *ibid.*, iii, 2, 14; *Sat.*, ii, 1,58.

7. "Augustus," *Carm.*, iii, 3, 11, 12; 25, 6; "adamant," *ibid.*, i, 6, 13; "sacred hill," *ibid.*, iv, 2, 35; "fetters," *Epod.*, vii, 8; "detested," *Carm.*, i, 37, 32; "asp," *ibid.*, i, 37, 28; "shepherd," *ibid.*, i, 15, 1, 2; "quieted waves," *ibid.*, i, 15, 3; "prophecy," *ibid.*, i, 15, 5; "Danae," *ibid.*, iii, 16; "royal maiden," *ibid.*, iii, 27, 25 ff.

8. "hags," *Epod.*, v; "herd," *Carm.*, ii, 16, 40; iii, 1, 1; "Lalage and wolf," *ibid.*, i, 22; "tree," *ibid.*, ii, 13; cf. ii, 17, 27; iii, 4, 27; 8, 8.

9. "fresh turf," *Carm.*, i, 1, 21; ii, 3, 6; *Epod.*, ii, 23; "springs," *Carm.*, i, 1, 22; *Epod.*, ii, 25 and 27; "birds," *ibid.*, ii, 26; "flowerets," *ibid.*, 19; "field," *ibid.*, 24; "lyre," *Carm.*, i, 1, 34; "India," *Epist.*, i, 1, 45; cf. *Carm.*, i, 31, 6; iii, 24, 2; "gleaming steeds," *Carm. Saec.* 9; "western Ocean," *Carm.*, i, 31, 14; *Epod.*, i, 13; "Islands of the Blessed," *Carm.*, iv, 8, 27; *Epod.*, xvi, 42; "Antium," *Carm.*, i, 35; "citadels," *ibid.*, ii, 6, 22; *Carm. Saec.*, 65; *Carm.*, i, 2, 3.

IX. TO PUBLIUS VERGILIUS MARO
(*Fam.*, XXIV, 11)

O illustrious Maro, bright luminary of eloquence and second hope of the Latian tongue,[1] fortunate Mantua rejoices in so great a son as thou, rejoices in having brought to light an ornament to the Roman name that will continue to adorn it throughout the centuries. What region of earth or what circle of Avernus arrests thee now? Does a swarthy Apollo play for thee on a harsh and grating lyre, and do the sable sisters now inspire thy verses? Dost thou soothe the Elysian groves with thy tender song, or dost thou dwell upon a Tartarean Helicon? And, O fairest of bards, does Homer, who was of one mind with thee, roam about in thy company? Orpheus and the other poets wander alone o'er the meadows, singing the praises of Phoebus—all except those whom a self-inflicted and violent death, or servile homage to a cruel lord has banished to other regions. Among them there is no place for Lucan, whom a cruel emperor drove to a wished-for death. His fear of torture and his abhorrence of a shameful death proved victorious, and he ordered the physician to open his veins.* A similar death took off Lucretius,³ whose savage fury (they say) compels him to dwell in far other regions than thou, Vergil.

And so, who are thy present companions? What life dost thou live? These are the questions I should gladly hear thee answer. And how near the truth were thy earthly dreams and imaginings? Hast thou been welcomed by the wandering Aeneas, and hast thou passed through the ivory portal by which he found exit?⁴ Or, rather, dost thou dwell in that quiet region of heaven which receives the blessed, where the stars smile benignly upon the peaceful shades of the illustrious? Wert thou received thither after the conquest of the Stygian abodes and the plundering of the Tartarean regions, on the arrival of that Highest King who, victorious in the great struggle, crossed the unholy threshold with pierced feet, and, irresistible, beat down the unyielding bars of hell with His pierced hands, and hurled its gates from their horrid-sounding hinges? All this should I like to learn from thee.

If the shade of anyone lately of this world of ours should perchance visit thee in the silent world, receive from him news which I have intrusted to him. Learn from him the present condition of three cities dear to thee, and the treatment which has been accorded to thy three works.

Parthenope is in grief. Widowed, she mourns the death of King Robert. One day has robbed her of the fruits of many years, and now her people are held in suspense and are threatened with an uncertain fate.⁵ The sins of the few are visited upon an innocent population. Mantua, best of cities, is ceaselessly tossed by the disturbances of her neighbors; but, shielding herself behind her great-souled leaders,⁶ she scorns to submit her unconquered head to the yoke, rejoicing in her own compatriot lords and ignorant of the rule of the stranger. It is in this city that I have composed what thou art now reading. It is here that I have found the friendly repose of thy rural fields. I constantly wonder by what path thou wert wont to seek the unfrequented glades in thy strolls, in what fields wert wont to roam, what streams to visit, or what recess in the curving shores of the lake, what shady groves and forest fastnesses. Constantly I wonder where it was that thou didst rest upon the sloping sward, or that, reclining in thy moments of fatigue, thou didst press with thy elbow upon the grassy turf or upon the marge of a charming spring. Such thoughts as these, O Vergil, bring thee vividly before my eyes.

Thou hast heard the fortune of thy native city, hast heard also what degree of peace hovers about thy grave. But what is taking place in Rome, our common mother—this, O Vergil, pray do not seek to know.' Believe me, 'tis better not to know. Lend thine ear, therefore, to more pleasing news and learn of the great success of thy works. Learn that Tityrus, though older, continues to blow upon the slender reed-pipe; that thy small holding is still joyful with its crops, thanks to thy fourfold work; that Aeneas lives, and gives pleasure with his song throughout the world. Yea, Aeneas lives, notwithstanding that death, envious of thy great and noble beginnings, overtook thee as thou wert so earnestly endeavoring to raise him to the skies. The Fates were on the point of fastening their clutches upon the unhappy Aeneas. Condemned by thine own lips, he was about to depart from us when once again the mercy of Augustus snatched him from these second flames, him who seemed destined to be destroyed by fire.[8] Augustus was not moved by the dejected spirits of his dying friend, and justly will he be praised by all succeeding generations for having disregarded thy last wishes. Farewell forever, O beloved one; and pray greet in my behalf thy elders, Homer and the Ascraean.

NOTES ON *Fam.*, XXIV, 11, TO VERGIL

1. An allusion by Petrarch to the statement which he himself makes in the second letter to Cicero, *Fam.*, XXIV, 4. (Consult n. 6 of that letter.)

2. St. Jerome, *Chron.*, (Migne, Vol. XXVII, coll. 453, 454): "M. Annaeus Lucan of Cordova, a poet, having been detected as participating in the conspiracy of Piso, held out his arm to the physician that his veins might be opened." This statement was taken from Suetonius (*Rel.*, p. 299, ll. 10-12 [Teubner]), who gives the further detail that Lucan committed suicide at the close of a splendid banquet— "epulatusque largiter" (*op. cit.*, p. 300, ll. 3, 4; Reifferscheid, *Rel.*, p. 52, ll. 1, 2). The statement of the commentator Vacca on the subject— "venas sibi praecidit" (Reiff., *op. cit.*, p. 78, l. 6)—cannot be considered the source of Petrarch's "arterias medico dedit ille cruento" (Vol. III, p. 291, l. 2), because the word "medicus" does not appear therein, as it does in the passage cited from St. Jerome (Suetonius).

3. Again St. Jerome is the authority. *Chron.*,

(Migne, Vol. XXVII, coll. 425, 426): "Titus Lucretius the poet is born, who in later years went mad because of a love philter. And although in the intervals of lucidity he composed several books (which Cicero afterward corrected), he committed suicide in the forty-fourth year of his age."

4. *Aeneid*, vi, 898, and Conington's translation, p. 215:

> Conversing still, the sire attends
> The travellers on their road,
> And through the ivory portal sends
> From forth the unseen abode.

5. Queen Joanna (the granddaughter and successor of King Robert, who died January 19, 1343) had been espoused while still a child to her cousin Andrew. The latter's manners were rough and uncouth and "more worthy of his native country, than of that polished court wherein he had been bred." After being tolerated for some time, he was one night seized, strangled, and thrown out of a window of the Castle of Aversa (September 18, 1345). Queen Joanna was at once accused of having been privy to the crime, although there was no actual proof to that effect. To avenge Andrew's death, his brother, Louis I the Great, king of Hungary

and Poland, successfully invaded the kingdom of Naples in the end of 1347. The Black Death obliged him to return to his own country the following year, whereupon Queen Joanna returned, and carried on a desultory warfare with the Hungarian party in Naples. In 1350 King Louis made a second expedition against Naples, but he soon found it more difficult to retain the kingdom than it had been to conquer it. And since affairs at home required his presence, he agreed to a treaty in 1351 and left Naples. The city was soon recovered by Queen Joanna (in 1352) whose reign continued for many years, undisturbed by any attack of a foreign enemy (Hallam, Vol. I, pp. 347, 348, and Lodge, *The Close of the Middle Ages*, pp. 152, 153). The period of suspense mentioned by Petrarch must, therefore, have been from the assassination of King Andrew (1345) to the treaty agreed upon in 1351, which accords fully with the date 1349 assigned to this letter by Fracassetti (Vol. 5, p. 182).

6. The family of the Gonzaga. After the murder of Rinaldo Buonacolsi (surnamed Passerino) and after the defeat of his followers (1328), Luigi Gonzaga became captain-general of Mantua. This dignity was confirmed as

a hereditary title by Louis IV of Bavaria, who in 1329 nominated him imperial vicar. Luigi thus became Louis I, the founder of a new ducal house which furnished the lords of Mantua uninterruptedly for four centuries. The direct line became extinct in 1708.

In 1348 the sons of Louis I of Mantua, Filippino and Guido, defeated the allied forces of the Visconti, Scaligeri, and Estensi, under the command of Lucchino Visconti at Borgoforte, a village fourteen kilometers south of Mantua, and beat back the Milanese a second time in 1357. The praise bestowed by Petrarch must have been due to the victory won by the Gonzaga in 1348. And a truly remarkable victory it was, considering the great success which attended the efforts of the Visconti to bring the ruling houses of Italy under the power of the Viper (cf. J. A. Symonds, *The Age of the Despots* [London 1897], pp. 113, 114).

7. Petrarch was most sadly disappointed in Rienzo's failure and the consequent anarchy at Rome.

> Rome was again agitated by the bloody feuds of the barons, who detested each other and despised the commons; their hostile fortresses, both in town and country, again rose and were again demolished; and the peaceful

citizens, a flock of sheep, were devoured, says the Florentine historian, by these rapacious wolves. But, when their pride and avarice had exhausted the patience of the Romans, a confraternity of the Virgin Mary protected or avenged the republic; the bell of the Capitol was again tolled, the nobles in arms trembled in the presence of an unarmed multitude; and of the two senators, Colonna escaped from the window of the palace, and Ursini was stoned at the foot of the altar" (Gibbon, Vol. VII, p. 276).

And with equal eloquence, Gregorovius exclaims (Vol. VI, Pt. I, pp. 318, 319):

The unlucky fugitive (Rienzo), however, cherished one satisfaction; this was the state of wild anarchy to which the city had reverted, after having enjoyed peace and order under his government. Disunion prevailed among both people and nobility; family wars both within and without; robbery and crime in every street.

8. The story of Vergil's dying wish to burn the *Aeneid* is well known. Petrarch learned it from Donatus. Also the statement concerning the command of Augustus is to be found in Donatus (*Vita Verg.*, XV, 56, p. 63 R), who cites the verses by Sulpicius containing the allusion to the rescue of the *Aeneid* from these "second flames" (*op. cit.*, 57, p. 63 R: "et paene est alio Troia cremata rogo." Compare Baehrens, *Poetae latini minores*, Vol. IV, p. 182,

No. 184, where the lines are ascribed to Servius Varius).

Petrarch, moreover, knew the story of the rescue also from the famous poem "Ergone supremis," to which he makes two distinct references: one in *Epistolae Poeticae*, II, 3, last 2 verses, *Opera*, III, p. 90 (P. de Nolhac, I, p. 125, n. 1, and Sabbadini, *Rend. del R. Ist. Lomb.*, [1906], p. 197); the other in a marginal note to Servius' life of Vergil, at the words "hac lege iussit emendare," where Petrarch says, "Super hoc elegantissimo carmine se excusans." This is a clear reference to the poem "Ergone supremis" (Sabbadini, *op. cit.*, p. 194).

This oft-mentioned poem is cited in the interpolated version of Donatus' life of Vergil (XV, 58, p. 63 R). But it has already been proved doubtful whether Petrarch was acquainted with this version. (See above, second letter to Cicero, n. 6.) Hence it is more probable that Petrarch knew the "Ergone supremis" directly from the *Anthologia* (Baehrens, *op. cit.*, Vol. IV, p. 179, No. 183, and Sabbadini, *op. cit.*, p. 198).

Petrarch knew of two additional sources for the story. He refers to Macrobius (I, 24, 6), in a marginal note to Servius' "praecepit incendi.

Augustus vero," saying, "de hoc Macrobio" (Sabbadini, *op. cit.*, p. 193). And lastly, though Petrarch nowhere makes direct reference to it, he may have used also Pliny, *N. H.*, vii, 30, 31.

Summary of sources in order of importance: Anthologia Latina, Macrobius, Donatus.

X. TO HOMER

(*Fam.*, XXIV, 12).

I have long desired to address thee in writing, and would have done so without hesitation if I had had a ready command of thy tongue. But alas! Fortune was unkind to me in my study of Greek.[1] Thou, on the other hand, seemest to have forgotten the Latin which it was formerly customary for our authors to bring to thy assistance, but which their descendants have failed to place at thy disposal.[2] And so, excluded from the one and the other means of communication, I kept my peace.

One man has once again restored thee to our age as a Latin.[3] Thy Penelope did not longer nor more anxiously await her Ulysses than I thee. My hopes, indeed, had been deserting me one by one. Excepting the opening lines of several books of thy poem,[4] wherein I beheld thee as one sees, from a distance, the doubtful and rapid look of a wished-for friend, or perhaps, catches a glimpse of his streaming hair—with this exception, then, no portion of thy works had come into my hands in Latin translation.

Nothing, in fine, warranted the hope that I might some day behold thee nigh at hand. For that little book which commonly passes as thine, though it is clearly taken from thee and is inscribed with thy name, is nevertheless not thine.⁵ Who the author of it may be is not certain. That other person (to whom I have already referred) will restore thee to us in thy entirety, if he lives.⁶ Indeed, he has already begun his task, in order that we may derive pleasure not merely from the excellent contents of thy divine poem, but also from the charms of conversing with thee. The Greek flavor has recently been enjoyed by me from a Latin flagon.⁷

This experience brought forcibly home to me the fact that a vigorous and keen intellect can all things. Cicero was, in many instances, merely an expounder of thy thoughts; Vergil was even more frequently a borrower; both, however, were the princes of the Latin speech. And though Annaeus Seneca assert that Cicero loses all his eloquence when dabbling in verse and that Vergil's felicity of expression deserts him when venturing into the realms of prose,⁸ still I maintain that it is but right that each of them be compared with himself and not with the other. From such comparison it would clearly result that each should be considered as having fallen below his own highest level. Judged by themselves, I insist that I have read verses of Cicero that are not mere doggerel, and prose letters of Vergil that are not disagreeable.[9]

I am now experiencing the same emotions in thy case, for thy great work, too, is a poetical masterpiece. In obedience to the maxim laid down by St. Jerome (a Latin author of exceptional skill in languages), I wrote once upon a time that if thou wert to be translated literally, not merely into Latin prose, but even into Greek prose, from being most eloquent of poets thou wouldst be made of none effect.[10] Now, on the contrary, thou dost still retain thy hidden power to please, though turned into prose, and what is more, into Latin prose.[11] This fact compels admiration. Whatever, therefore, may be said of me, let no one marvel that I have addressed Vergil in verse, but thee in the more tractable and yielding prose.[12] Him I addressed of my own free will; in thy case, I am answering a letter received.[13] Furthermore, with Vergil I employed the idiom which we possessed in common; with thee I have adopted, not thy ancient language, but a certain new speech in which the letter I received was couched, a speech which I use daily, but which is not, I suppose, the one to which thou art accustomed.

But after all, why should I dignify my talk with both of you by giving it the name conversation? Our very best must appear to you mere prattle and chattering. Ye are unapproachable; ye are more than mortal, and your heads pierce the clouds. Yet it is with me as with a babe: I love to babble with those who feed me, even though they are skilled masters of speech. But enough on the subject of style. I now come to the contents of thy letter.

Thou dost complain of several things, and as a matter of fact thou couldst with almost perfect justice complain of everything. What in this world, pray, can escape just complaint? This exception, however, must be borne in mind: the moment laments begin to be ineffectual, they somehow cease to be justifiable. Thy grievances, indeed, do not lack a just cause, but they are without their desired effect, which is that, while condemning the past, they should provide some remedy for the present and make some provision for the future. Considering, however, that the expression of our grievances does in truth relieve the burden of our sorrow for the time being, clamoring cannot be said to be altogether of no avail. At present, O great one, thy soul is overburdéned with grief. Thy long letter is one connected series of complaints, and yet I would it had been longer. Only tediousness and lack of interest can cause anything to seem long.

Permit me, now, to touch briefly upon the various details. What thou didst write of thy teachers filled me, who am so greedy for knowledge and learning, with boundless and incredible joy. Hitherto, I confess, they were absolutely unknown to me; but hereafter, thanks to their renowned disciple, they will be honored and worshiped by me. Thy letter touches upon matters entirely new to us: on the origin of poetry, which thou dost trace to its most ancient sources; on the earliest followers of the Muses, among whom, in addition to the well-known dwellers upon Helicon, thou dost class Cadmus son of Agenor, and a certain Hercules, whether Alcides or not appears doubtful. I am glad to receive knowledge concerning the city of thy birth; for we had cloudy and hazy views thereupon, and (I see) even you Greeks were none too clear of the subject."⁴ Furthermore, thou dost describe thy pilgrimages undertaken in search of knowledge into Phoenicia and Egypt whither, several centuries afterward, the illustrious philosophers Pythagoras and Plato journeyed, and he who gave laws to the Athenians and who later in life became a devotee of the Pierides, the learned and venerable Solon. During life he was a great admirer of thine, and after death he must have become thy very intimate friend. Finally, thou dost inform us of the number of thy books, many of which were unknown even to the Italians, thy nearest neighbors. As to these barbarians by whom we are encircled —and I would that we were cut off from them, not merely by the lofty Alps, but indeed by the whole expanse of the broad ocean—as to these barbarians, they have not heard of thy name even, much less of the number of thy books. Let this serve as a proof unto men of how evanescent a dream is fame, for which we toil so breathlessly.

Thou didst add a very sad and bitter touch to so much that was truly pleasing, when thou didst mention the loss of those same books. Oh unhappy me, thrice unhappy! How many, many things are lost! Nay, all things perish—all that our own blind activity accomplishes 'neath the course of the ever-returning sun. Vain are the labors and cares of men! Time flies, and, short as it is, we waste it. Oh, the vanity and pride of men over the nothingness that we are and do and hope for! Who will now place confidence in a dim ray of light? The supreme Sun of eloquence has himself suffered eclipse. Who will now dare to mourn the partial loss of his own works? Who will now dare cherish the hope that any fruit of his labors will endure forever?

The fruits of Homer's sleepless toil have perished in large measure. Not ours the fault, for no one can lose that which he does not possess. The Greeks themselves are to blame. That they might not yield the palm to us in any phase of life whatsoever, they have exceeded even our sloth and neglect in the domain of letters, and have suffered themselves to lose many of Homer's books, which were to them as so many rays of glory. Such blindness makes them unworthy of the boast that they once produced so luminous a star.

Again, I was deeply stirred by what thou didst relate concerning thy end. Even among us the accepted story of thy death was widespread. I myself gave it currency on occasion, adhering to the common version, 'tis true, but yet adding to it a note of uncertainty.[15] For it gave me pleasure, and (with thy kind leave) it still gives me pleasure, to entertain a better opinion of thee and of Sophocles.[16] I am unwilling to believe that grief and joy—those most disturbing passions of the mind—could have held such powerful sway over such divine intellects. Similarly, if we are to believe common hearsay, Philemon died of laughter. But we have at last become acquainted with a more serious and more credible version: that his death followed a period of unconsciousness due, not to excessive laughter (as report would have it), but to the wasting and sapping effects of a most profound meditation.[17]

But to return to thee alone and to thy death—how violent and how lengthy are thy lamentations! Calm thyself, I beg of thee. Thou wilt succeed, I am sure, if thou wilt banish thy passions and return to thy proper self. Much dost thou complain of thy imitators, much of those who scoffed at and reviled thee. Just complaints these, if, indeed, thou wert the only one to suffer such treatment; if scoffing and reviling were vices unknown to man, instead of their being (as they surely are,) well-worn and common traits. Hence it is that thou must fain bow to the inevitable—thou who art the foremost of this class, I grant thee, but yet not a class in thyself.

What, in truth, am I to say on this subject? When thou didst behold thyself soaring so high on the wings of fancy, thou shouldst have foreseen that thou wouldst never lack imitators. Surely it must be gratifying to thee that many should wish to resemble thee. Very few, however, find it possible. Forsooth, why shouldst thou not rejoice, conscious as thou art of ever holding the first place? Even I, the least among men, not only rejoice, but, as if rejoicing were not sufficient, glory and boast that I am now held in such esteem that some (if some there be) hope to follow in my footsteps and to fashion as I have fashioned. Indeed, my joy would be the greater were my imitators such as ultimately to surpass me. I do not address my vows to that Apollo of thine; but I pray and beseech my God, the true God of genius, to grant that, if there be anyone who has deemed me a worthy pattern to follow, he may overtake me with easy efforts and indeed outstrip me. I shall consider that I have wrought gloriously and effectively if I discover among my friends many who are my equals—and I call them friends because no one will desire to model himself after me unless he love me. Still more fortunate shall I deem myself if I recognize superiors among those who, having been content to follow for a time, later lead the way as conquerors. For if a father desires that the child of his flesh and blood be greater than himself, what should the author wish for the child of his intellect? And since thou canst entertain no fear of a greater or superior, bear with thy imitators patiently and calmly.

In the books of the *Saturnalia* there is an unsettled discussion on the question of superiority between thee and that one of whom thou dost complain so bitterly, Vergil.[18] There are some among us who consider the issue a doubtful one; others award the crown to Vergil without hesitation. I tell thee this, not because I favor or oppose the one or the other judgment, but that thou mayst know what and how varying opinions posterity holds of thee.

And here, O best of leaders, my conscience bids me, before proceeding farther, to undertake the defense of Vergil himself—a soul (as Flaccus says)[19] the like of which this earth has ne'er produced more spotless. What thou didst say of his imitating thee is not merely true, but forms part of common knowledge. Moreover, many other true things might have been said by thee, but respect (or was it modesty?) forbade. Thou wilt find all the various points discussed in order in the *Saturnalia*. There too thou wilt find the sharp retort of Vergil, who, when charged by his rivals with having stolen verses from thee, answered that it was a sign of great power to wrest the club from the hands of Hercules.[20] I am quite certain that thou wilt detect the veiled pungency of this witticism.

I by no means intend to incriminate him whom I set out to defend, as so many do. I frankly admit the truth of all thou sayest. Still, I cannot listen calmly to thy complaint, when thou sayest that though Vergil is overladen and bedecked with thy spoils he nowhere deigns to make mention of thy name. Thou dost adduce the opposite case of Lucan (and with perfect right) who in grateful words acknowledges his indebtedness to the bard of Smyrna.[21] Let me add further instances in favor of thy side. Flaccus frequently refers to thee, and always in noble words; for on one occasion he exalts thee above the philosophers themselves, and on another he assigns to thee the most honored seat among the poets." Naso mentions thee, and Juvenal, and Statius. But why should I rehearse the long list of those who make mention of thee? Practically not a single one of our authors has been thus forgetful.

Why then, thou wilt say, should I bear the ingratitude of him alone who deservedly should have been the most grateful of all? Before answering, let me heap coals of fire on thy wounded feelings. Do not by any mischance suppose that Vergil was similarly ungrateful to all. Know that he mentions—and not once merely—Musaeus and Linus and Orpheus; and what is more, that he pays the greatest deference to the poets Hesiod the Ascraean and Theocritus the Syracusan. Finally, he does not omit mention even of Varus and Gallus and of other contemporaries—a thing which jealousy would never have permitted, had he harbored such base feeling.

What now? Do I not seem to have aggravated the causes of that plaint which I had proposed to lessen or entirely to remove? Yes, if I were to stop at this point. But thou must hear me out. We must examine all the circumstances and bring to bear all our reasoning faculties, especially since we are to sit as judges.

Vergil naturally makes mention of Theocritus in the *Bucolics*, because he had taken him as his model; and likewise, in the appropriate place in the *Georgics*, he speaks of Hesiod." And then thou wilt ask, "Why does he make no mention of me anywhere in his heroic poem, seeing that he had chosen me as his third model?" Believe me, Homer; had not wicked death prevented, Vergil would have given thee due honor, for he was the most gentle and modest of men, and (as we read) a man of irreproachable life. Others he honored when the opportunity presented itself and in those places where it suited his convenience. For thee, to whom he was most heavily in debt, he was reserving a place, not selected by circumstances, but destined and marked out after due deliberation. Which place, dost thou suppose? Which but the most distinguished and conspicuous? The end of his illustrious poem it was that he had reserved for thee. There he had destined to hail thee as his leader and in sonorous lines to exalt thy name to the stars. What place more worthy, I ask, in which to praise the leader of our journey? Thou hast good cause, therefore, for mourning the over-early death which cut off Vergil, and the Italian world shares thy grief; but thou canst have no grievances against thy friend.

I shall cite a very close and similar example to prove the truth of my previous remarks. Even as Vergil took thee as his model, so he in his turn was chosen by Papinius Statius, whom I have mentioned above, a man renowned not merely for his intellectual powers but also for the singular charm of his manners. And still he did not acknowledge the great leader of his genius until the end of his poetical journey. For, though he had already and in a less conspicuous place declared himself inferior to Vergil in style, it was only at the close that he openly and in good faith paid the full debt of his grateful soul to the author of the *Aeneid*."[4] If, then, death had untimely laid its hands upon Statius, Vergil also would have been unsung by his grateful follower, even as thou by him.

I should wish thee to be persuaded that it is as I say. For it is surely so, unless I am deceived by false signs; and even if it were otherwise, the more favorable of two opinions is the one to be preferred when in doubt. All the arguments I have advanced thus far are, of course, in extenuation of the chief works of Vergil. For if thou turnest thy attention to the short poems which are called his earlier works—clearly his first youthful efforts—thou wilt there find mention of thy name."⁵

It now remains for me to touch lightly upon the minor complaints scattered here and there throughout the body of thy letter. Thou grievest that thou hast been mangled and dismembered by thy imitators. It had needs be so, Homer. No man's intellect was sufficiently vigorous to grasp thee whole. Thou dost wax indignant, moreover, that they should shower abuse upon thee though clothed in thy spoils."⁶ Alas! it is only what thou must expect; no one can be particularly ungrateful except him who has previously been the recipient of a great boon. Thy next charge is that, whereas thy name was held in great honor by the early jurists and physicians, to their successors it has become a subject of mockery and contempt. Thou dost not observe how different the later generations are from the preceding. If they were of a like stamp, they would love and cherish the same things. Let thy indignation cease, and thy sorrow as well. On the contrary, take comfort in hoping for the best. To be in disfavor with the wicked and the ignorant is the first sign of virtue and intelligence. The radiance of thy genius is so brilliant that our weak sight cannot endure it. It is with thee as with the sun, for which it is not reckoned a disgrace but praise most high, that it conquers the vision of the weak and puts to flight the birds of night. Among the ancients, and indeed also among men of today—if any there are in whom there still lives even a small spark of our early nature—thou must be esteemed not merely a holy philosopher (as thou thyself sayest") but greater and superior to any philosopher, as I have said above."[8] Thou dost cover a most beautiful philosophy with a very charming and transparent veil.

Assuredly thou canst have no concern for the disesteem in which thou art held by the monstrous men of today. Indeed, it is most earnestly to be desired that thou shalt continue to displease them, for this is the first step to glory. The second step is not to have one's merits acknowledged. Dismiss therefore, I beg of thee, all care and sorrow, and return to that deserved seat of honor in the Elysian Fields which thou didst formerly hold and whence thou sayest thou wert driven by such trifling absurdities. It is not fitting that the composure of the sage should be dispelled by the affronts of fools. Otherwise what would be the result? What would ever put an end to the evil, since the Hebrew philosopher most verily hath said, "The number of fools is infinite"?[29] No truer word could have been spoken. Do not all the streets and homes and public squares attest it?

Thy next grievance is, to my mind, a cause for great joy and for sincere happiness, though thou seemest to be so enraged by it. Even sweets taste bitter to him who has a disordered stomach. Thou dost weep when it had been more appropriate to rejoice. Thou dost weep because our common friend (whom thou takest to be a Thessalian and whom I have always thought a Byzantine[30]) has compelled thee to enter within the walls of my flourishing native city, to live among strangers or (if thou dost insist) to live the life of an exile. Rest assured that he has done and is doing so in the greatest good faith and out of sincerest love for thee. By his labor he has commenced to endear himself to all who cherish thy name, and who, though few in number, still do exist. See to it, therefore, that thou dost not nourish any resentment against that very person to whom we—lovers all of thee—are giving thanks both in our name and in thine. If fortune befriend his undertaking, he will restore thee to us and to the Ausonian Muses, who have so long been seeking to know thee.

Cease wondering that the valley of Fiesole and the banks of the Arno can boast of but three who are thy friends. It is enough; it is much; yes, it is more than I had hoped for, to have found three Pierian spirits in a city so given over to Mammon. But do not despair. The city is a large and populous one; seek and thou wilt find a fourth. To these I should add a fifth—for he surely deserves it—him I mean whose brow was garlanded with the Penean or Alphean laurels. But I know not how it is that we have been deprived of him by the Babylon across the Alps. Does it seem to thee nothing wonderful to encounter five such men at one time and in one city? Seek elsewhere, and what hast thou? That famous Bologna for which thou dost sigh, most generous seat of learning as it is, can produce but one, though thou shouldst search it from end to end. Verona boasts of two, and Sulmona of one. Also Mantua might vaunt of one, if his theological studies did not draw him away from earthly matters;

for he has deserted thy ensigns and has ranged himself beneath those of Ptolemy. Wonderful to relate, Rome herself, the head and center of all things, has been drained of such citizens almost to a man. Perugia did have one who gave great promise of the future, but he neglected opportunities for developing his better self. He has abandoned not only Parnassus, but the Apennines and the Alps as well, and is now, in his old age, roaming about Spain, scratching away at parchments to earn his livelihood as a scribe. Other cities gave birth to other friends of thine, but all whom I became acquainted with have departed from this mortal habitation for that universal and eternal city."[31] This, then, is what I am leading up to: that thou shouldst not continue to complain of one who is indeed thy friend, since he has brought thee to a country boasting of only a few friends and admirers, it is true, but still of more such than thou wouldst find today in any other land.

Art thou, perchance, unaware how few scholars there have been at all times, even in our country? Unless I am mistaken, this same friend of ours is at this time the only scholar in all Greece. My late teacher was a second.[32] But alas! he died after having raised within me most pleasing hopes of ultimate success, leaving me at the mere threshold of such studies. Indeed, even before his death he had left me to shift for myself; for, having regard for his rather than for my own advantage, I had added my influence to procure his elevation to a bishopric. Therefore, Homer, bear up with this small handful of followers and grant to an enfeebled and declining age the same indulgence which thou wouldst have granted to a strong and flourishing one.

Formerly there were a few who highly valued the ennobling study of letters. Today their number is sadly diminished, and I predict that shortly they will have disappeared entirely."[33] It is best to abide with these few as eagerly as may be, and pray do not for one instant harbor the thought of exchanging our stream for any larger channel. Thou art no mere mariner, nor fisherman; nay, if the report be true (and I would it were false) thy intercourse with that tribe was none too auspicious.[34] The small Castalian fount and the low and humble Helicon once did give thee pleasure. May our Arno and our hills be as fortunate, where noble intellects abound like the gushing waters of the hills and where the sweetly singing nightingales build their nests. These are few indeed, I confess; but to repeat, if thou surveyest the land far and near, they will appear relatively many. Outside of these few singers what dost thou hope to find in our population except fullers, weavers, and smiths? Not to mention impostors, whom wilt thou come upon except publicans, thieves of various kinds, thousands of frauds and cheats, hostile factions that never hesitate to resort to deceitful means, the anxious avaricious and their vain struggles, and the rank scum that pursues the mechanical trades? Among such as these thou must needs endure all scoffing with unruffled brow, as an eagle among the night-owls, as a lion among apes. In their presence thou must repeat what Ennius, greatly thy inferior, once said: "I flit about in life on the lips of (learned) men."[35] Let the lips of the untaught continue to disclose their ignorance and utter vain gossip. Let them remain in ignorance of thee and thy works, or, knowing, let them revile. Praise from such lips would be blasphemy indeed.

I come now to myself, so that, being the least in intellect and in years, I may also form the last topic of my letter. In thy adversity thou dost beg me to come to thy aid. Oh, cruel and inexorable fate! In succoring so great a man as thou I could forever boast of a better claim to glory than any I have yet attained or hope to attain. I call Christ to witness—a God to thee unknown—that there is absolutely nothing which I can offer for thy relief except affectionate, tender pity and loyal advice. What assistance, indeed, can be received from one who can do nothing for himself? Hast thou not heard that even thy followers were reviled out of hatred for thy name, and that they were judged insane by an assembly of insane? If this could happen in thine own age and in Athens, most cultured of cities, what dost thou suppose will be the case today with other poets in cities entirely devoted to the pursuit of pleasure? I am one of those at whom the vulgar and the ignorant aim their shafts. I am astonished and wonder why it is so. If only I had given cause for some justifiable hatred! But it matters not how just the cause may or may not have been; the reality of their hatred is undeniable. And is it on my bosom, then, that thou wouldst seek refuge? Oh, insensate turn of fortune's wheel! No palace could be sufficiently spacious and resplendent for thee, Homer, if great intellects were to strive for such material honors as fortune can bestow. But not so: genius spurns the turrets and castles of the ignorant, and delights in the lonely and lowly hut. For my part, although I do not consider myself worthy of so great a guest, I have already harbored thee at my home both in Greek and (as far as it was possible) in Latin.³⁶ I trust to have thee entire before long, provided thy Thessalian will complete what he has begun.³⁷ Know, however, that thou art to be received in an even more sacred inclosure: I have made preparations to welcome thee with the greatest eagerness and devotion to the innermost recesses of my heart. In a word, my love for thee is greater and warmer than the rays of the sun, and my esteem such that no one could cherish a greater.

This is all I have been able to offer thee, leader and father. Any attempt to free thee from the scorn of the rabble would result in detracting from thy singular and peculiar praise. Moreover, it is a task beyond my powers and those of any other, except perhaps of that man who will have sufficient strength to curb the passions of the mob. And although God has such power, He has not exerted it in the past, nor do I think He is likely to do so hereafter.

I have spoken at great length as if thou wert

present. Emerging now from those very vivid flights of the imagination, I realize how very far removed thou art, and I fear lest it may be annoying to thee to read so lengthy a letter in the dim light of the lower world. I reassure myself when I remember that also thy letter was long.

Farewell forever. And when thou wilt have returned to thy seat of honor, pray give kindly greetings to Orpheus, Linus, Euripides, and the rest.

Written in the world above, in that city lying between the famous rivers Po, Ticino, Adda, and others, whence some say Milan derives its name, on the ninth of October in the thirteen hundred and sixtieth year of this last era.

Notes on *Fam.*, XXIV, 12, to Homer

1. The man who taught Petrarch the elements of Greek was Bernardo Barlaamo, theologian, mathematician, astronomer, and philosopher. This learned Italian monk was born at Seminara, Calabria Ulteriore, and entered the Roman Catholic monastery of St. Basil. From Calabria he journeyed to Aetolia, afterward studied at Thessalonica (at that time a center of learning), and finally (1327 or 1328) went to Constantinople, the better to learn Greek and thus be able to read Aristotle in the original. He at once became a member of the Greek church, and in 1331 was appointed Abbot of the Convent of St. Salvator at Constantinople. He was protected by Andronicus III (Palaeologus, 1328-41), who in 1339 sent him to Avignon on a diplomatic mission to Pope Benedict XII, endeavoring to bring about the union of the two churches in common cause against the Turks. In this mission Barlaamo was unsuccessful. Returning to Greece, he attacked the Hesychasts (or Quietists) of Mt. Athos, and became involved with Gregory

Palamas (afterward archbishop of Thessalonica) on the question of the light which had been manifested to the disciples on Mt. Tabor at the Transfiguration. At a synod held at Constantinople in 1341, the Hesychasts defended themselves so ably that Barlaamo was condemned. Since his protector was now dead, he was compelled to flee into Italy.

He at once re-entered the Roman church and was made librarian by King Robert. In 1342 he revisited Avignon on a second mission, and it is on this occasion that he must have made the acquaintance of Petrarch (P. de Nolhac, II, p. 136), who during the summer of 1342 received from him daily instruction in Greek— whether at Avignon or at Vaucluse is not clear. At the end of the summer Petrarch had made but small progress. Still he added his recommendation to those of others when Pope Clement VI nominated Barlaamo bishop of Gerace, a town in Calabria sixty miles northeast of Reggio. He was consecrated bishop at Avignon on October 2, 1342, and thereafter left for Gerace, dying in that town six years later, in 1348.

In conclusion, then, the first seeds of Greek in the West were sown by a learned, ambitious

Calabrian monk, who (to use a modern expression) went abroad to complete his education, committed apostasy to further his ambition, repeating the act fourteen years later when defeated in a religious controversy; a man who, though born in Italy, was more Greek than Roman (to the extent of almost forgetting his Latin), who never had entertained the remotest idea of being a teacher of Greek, and who cared very little for the humble pupil offered him by chance at Avignon—the enthusiastic poet and scholar who had received the Laurel Crown at Rome the year before, and who was destined to become known to future generations as the "first modern scholar."

2. A reference to the translation of the *Odyssey* made by Livius Andronicus, and to the *Epitome* of the *Iliad*, which is now attributed to Silius Italicus, but which in the Middle Ages was known as the *Homerus Latinus* and later as the *Pindarus Thebanus* (see n. 5).

3. The allusion is to Leonzio Pilato, who claimed to be a pupil of Barlaamo. The place of his birth is uncertain, owing to the peculiar character of the man. He was never content with his actual position and surroundings. In consequence, when in Italy he disdained and

reviled the Italians and things Italian, and declared himself a native of Thessalonica—as if (comments Petrarch) it were more honorable to be of Greek than of Italian origin. Similarly, when in Greece he could not find anyone or anything praiseworthy in the Eastern Empire and in Byzantium, but boasted of his Calabrian origin. The probability is that he was born in Calabria. The date is unknown.

Authorities differ as the to year when Leonzio became acquainted with Petrarch (see n. 6). Accordingly, the long-bearded adventurer is said to have met Petrarch at Padua during the winter of 1358–59. The poet immediately grasped the opportunity of having him translate some passages from the manuscript of Homer which had been sent to him by Sigero in 1354 (P. de Nolhac, II, p. 156). In March, 1359, Petrarch received a visit at Milan from Boccaccio, and may have introduced Leonzio to him (Koerting, *Boccaccio*, p. 261). Doubtless Petrarch told him of his recent acquaintance (P. de Nolhac, *ibid.*, p. 157), and showed him the specimen translations from the *Iliad* which had been made in the winter just passed (*ibid.*, p. 173, and n. 4 below). Leonzio, it appears, had in the meantime roved to Venice, where the anxious Boccaccio overtook him (Koerting, *op. cit.*, p. 260). Shortly afterward Leonzio declared his intention of leaving for Avignon in search of fortune. But so desirous was Boccaccio of learning Greek, and so eager, therefore, to have him near at hand, that he prevailed upon the Calabrian to visit Florence, which city they reached together in the early part of 1360; for in August of that year Leonzio had already been some time at Florence (Koerting, *ibid.*). There Boccaccio gave him lodging at his own home, and exerted all his influence to have him appointed professor at the Studio Fiorentino. His efforts were crowned with success, for the Republic decided to pay Leonzio an annual stipend in return for his services, which were to consist in giving public lectures on the works of Homer. Thus was established the first chair of Greek in the West, and Leonzio Pilato, adventurer though he was, has the honor of being the first professor of the Greek language and literature in a western university. He held the newly established chair of Greek from 1360 to 1363. During three years, from the summer of 1359 to November, 1361 (Koerting, *op. cit.*, p. 262), the author of the *Decam-*

eron and the other two Florentine friends of Homer alluded to by Petrarch took private lessons of Leonzio with great eagerness, and we can readily picture them in Boccaccio's library, sitting at the feet of the Calabrian and drinking "the muddy stream of pseudo-learning and lies that flowed from this man's lips, with insatiable avidity" (J. A. Symonds, *The Revival of Learning*, p. 67, ed. 1898).

It goes without saying that Petrarch was kept duly informed by Boccaccio of affairs at Florence. The question of translating Homer was of course uppermost in the minds of both these early humanists, and it was broached the moment Pilato became established at the university. Strange to relate, a good manuscript of Homer was not to be had at Florence, and even Leonzio does not seem to have had one in his possession. Boccaccio, however, had been told that there was such a manuscript for sale at Padua, and so wrote to Petrarch requesting him to procure it. Petrarch promised to do so, adding that if the Paduan volume slipped through their hands, he would be happy to place at Leonzio's disposal the copy sent to him in 1354 by Sigero. And here it is best to listen to the words of Petrarch himself on the subject.

In a letter dated at Milan, August 18, 1360 (*Var.*, 25), he says:

I now come to the last point—namely, that if (as you seem to think) I have bought the copy of Homer which was for sale at Padua, I should please to lend it to you. You reason that I possess another copy of old, and that you would entrust the new copy to our Leonzio to have him translate it from the Greek into Latin for the benefit of yourself and our other studious fellow-countrymen. I examined that copy, but did not give it a second thought because it was clearly inferior to mine. It may still be easily obtained through him who made me acquainted with that same Leonzio. Leonzio's letters will surely have great weight with him, and I shall write to him also. If the Paduan volume slips through our hands (which, however, I do not think likely) then mine will be at your service. I have always been very eager for translations of all the Greek authors, but of that one author in particular. Had Fate smiled more kindly upon me when I entered upon the student's career, and had not death so untimely overtaken my illustrious teacher, I should today, perhaps, have something more than a rudimentary knowledge of Greek. You may count upon me in your undertaking. Indeed, I grieve and am indignant at the loss of that ancient translation (the work of Cicero, as far as we can judge), the beginning of which Horace inserted in his poem on the *Ars Poetica* (vss. 141, 142). I can scarcely endure this neglect of the more truly precious things when I observe the eager pursuit of our age for those things that are low and base. But what am I to do? I must needs endure it. If proper care and diligence on the part of foreigners can in any way make amends for our own disregard, may the Muses and Apollo prosper their undertakings. Believe me, I could receive no more valuable nor acceptable merchandise either from the Chinese, or the Arabs, or from the shores of the Red Sea. Do not be shocked—I know what I am saying. I am fully aware that the nominative case I employed for the expression "acceptable merchandise" ("merx gratior") is not in common use with our grammarians. In the ancient writers, however, it is common. I do not mean merely those earlier authors, in whose footsteps the ignorant ones of today hesitate to follow. I have in mind those authors who are very near to us in time, but who in learning and intellect are vastly our superiors, men from whose merits the vain chattering and the blind pride of our age have not yet dared to detract. It is in these authors, I say, that the nominative case is found; and since the name occurs to me, I shall add that it is to be found in Horace. Let us, therefore, bring it again into good repute, if we can, and let us dare to recall from unworthy exile a word which has been banished from the domains of that tongue to the study of which we devote all our energies.

I should like to clear my conscience on one point, lest at some future day I may repent of having kept silent. You tell me that the translation will be a prose one and that it will also be very literal. If this be so, pray give due attention to the following passage from St. Jerome. I shall quote his exact words, because he had an intimate knowledge of both Latin and Greek, and was especially skilled in the art of translation. In the preamble to his Latin version of the *De temporibus* (a work by Eusebius of Caesarea), St. Jerome says; "If there is anyone who does not believe that the grace of the original is lost in translation, let him endeavor to translate Homer into Latin literally. I shall say more: let him translate Homer into the prose of his own vernacular, and he will recognize that the order of the words has rendered his translation ridiculous and that he has made the most eloquent and vigorous of poets of none effect." I have ventured to give you this warning now, that no labor nor time may be wasted. And yet, I greatly desire the thing done, no matter how. So ardently do I long to become acquainted with noble works that, as in the case of a famishing man, I do not insist on the art of a *chef*. I await therefrom with great expectations food for the soul. Some time ago Leonzio himself made for me a short translation, into Latin prose, of the beginning of Homer, which gave me a taste of the character of the whole work. The lines gave me pleasure even though they were proof of St. Jerome's assertion. After all, you see, they retained their hidden power to please; like unto certain rich foods which should be served in gelatine, but in which the efforts of the cook have not been crowned with success. The form may have been destroyed, but the taste and the odor do not perish.

Let Leonzio therefore persevere in his undertaking, and with the help of God may he restore to us Homer, who, as far as we are concerned, is a lost author. As regards the other Greek authors, may Heaven assist him in his labors. Both of you ask that I send you the volume of Plato which I managed to rescue from the fire of my transalpine retreat. Your zeal is most commendable and you will receive the volume in good time. You may rely upon it, no obstacle to your noble undertakings will ever be interposed by me. Be very careful, however, of one thing: do not commit the serious error of gathering within the covers of one and the same volume these two great princes of Greek thought. The weight of two such intellects would be too great for human shoulders to bear. Let Leonzio commence his task with the help of God; and of the two authors he has chosen to translate, let him begin with him who wrote so many centuries earlier. Farewell.

The Paduan volume must after all have gotten into Boccaccio's hands, for we know that Petrarch retained his own copy while Leonzio was engaged on the translation. Furthermore, from the date of the present letter addressed to Homer, October 9, 1360, we gather that Leonzio must have begun his task at least as early as October, 1360. From this date to 1363 he was occupied in translating both the *Iliad* and the *Odyssey*, a translation which Fracassetti (Vol. 4, pp. 96, 97) and P. de Nolhac (II, pp. 161–63) argue was made at Petrarch's expense. As to its merits it may be said that, like the one of Livius Andronicus, it was roughly made and was almost verbatim. The charlatan professor, it appears, knew but little of either Greek or Latin; and only on the score of relative knowledge and ignorance can we explain the implicit confidence placed in him by Boccaccio and by Petrarch. (For the opening lines of the *Iliad* and the *Odyssey* as translated by Leonzio, with references, consult Voigt, II, p. 111, n. 4, and J. A. Symonds, *Revival*, p. 68, ed. 1898.)

4. We have already seen that when Leonzio Pilato met Petrarch at Padua in the winter of 1358–59, the latter had him translate several portions of Homer (see n. 3, par. 2). It is to this translation that Petrarch here alludes (P. de Nolhac, II, p. 157, n. 2), for there is no evidence that Pilato sent him any specimens of the translations done at Florence (cf. Voigt, II, p. 111). Consequently, this too must be the allusion in the sentence occurring shortly below, "The Greek flavor has recently been enjoyed by me from a Latin flagon," and in the passage from *Var.* 25 (quoted in n. 3), "Some time ago Leonzio himself made for me a short translation, into Latin prose, of the beginning of Homer, which gave me a taste of the character of the whole work."

Further proof is offered by the marginal notes which Petrarch made to the text of Pilato's translation which Boccaccio sent him. Frequently he states that elsewhere a different rendering is made of the original, and even gives the variant. From a study of these P. de Nolhac concludes (II, pp. 171–74) that the variants derive from the translation made by Pilato at Padua in the winter of 1358–59; and that this earlier translation included, perhaps, only the first five books of the *Iliad*. This last fact serves to explain completely the expression used by Petrarch in the present letter, "praeter enim aliquot tuorum principia librorum" (Vol. III, p. 293).

5. Before Leonzio completed his translation (which was neither poetical nor Latin: Voigt, II, p. 191), Petrarch and other mediaeval students were obliged to content themselves with the *Periochae* of the *Iliad* and the *Odyssey* which are attributed to Ausonius, and with a poor *Epitome* of the *Iliad* which was known as the *Homerus Latinus* or *Pindarus Thebanus* (P. de Nolhac, II, p. 131). It is because of the existence of this that some maintain that Leonzio's was not the first Latin translation of modern times. A mere glance, however, will convince anyone that this *Homerus* (published in 1881 by Baehrens under the title "Italici Ilias Latina," in *Poetae latini minores*, Vol. III, pp. 7–59 inclusive), is not a real translation and does not correspond to the real Homer.

The poem consists of 1,070 hexameters, which were written while Nero was still ruling. It was quoted as early as Lactantius (died 325 A. D.), and was at first referred to by the simple designation *Homerus* or *Homerus Latinus*. The worthy monks of the Middle Ages, having read that Homer was a Greek, later felt it incumbent upon them to assign an author to this Latin version, and by some mysterious process they hit upon the "philosopher" Pindarus of Thebes. From the thirteenth century on, the name *Pindarus* prevailed.

In 1880 Fr. Buecheler observed that ll. 1-8 and 1063-70 of the *Ilias Latina* formed acrostics, reading respectively "Italicus" and "Scripsit" (*Rh.M.*, XXXV, p. 391). Hence he deduced that the *Epitome* was composed by Silius Italicus, the author of the *Punica*, who died in 101 A. D. This conclusion is practically accepted by Teuffel, who says (par. 320, nn. 7 and 8) that the *Ilias* is probably an early work of Silius Italicus. Baehrens (*op. cit.*) is more guarded, saying that it was written by a "certain Italicus" ("confecit .... Italicus quidam"), adding farther down on the same page (p. 3) that Buecheler's conclusion is not quite right ("minus recte"), simply because it has been proved that the *Ilias* was written under Nero, if not earlier. But since Nero died in 68 A. D., and Italicus in 101 A. D. (at the age of 75), it does not seem improbable that the *Ilias* does after all represent an early work, perhaps even exercise, of Silius Italicus.

It is a sign of keen and clear judgment on the part of Petrarch, to call into question both here and elsewhere (cf. *Fam.*, X, 4), in spite of his ignorance of the original, the real merits and the authenticity of the *Homerus Latinus*, in an age when it was universally accepted as a good and faithful translation from the Greek.

6. It seems à propos briefly to relate here Leonzio's career subsequent to the professorship at Florence and to the translation of Homer. Upon invitation of Niccoló Acciaiuoli, a Florentine who then held the post of grand seneschal at the court of Naples, Boccaccio had paid a visit to that city in 1361 (Koerting, *Bocc.*, p. 262), taking Leonzio as his traveling companion. Leaving in the beginning of the summer of 1363, the two paid Petrarch a visit at Venice; and it is from this visit that some would date the beginning of Leonzio's personal acquaintance with Petrarch (Frac., 4, p. 97). Boccaccio spent the months of June, July, and August,

1363, at Venice with his dearly beloved friend, but was then obliged to return to the city on the Arno. He wished Leonzio to accompany him as before; but such was the inconstancy of that gloomy Calabrian that he absolutely refused to do so, declaring his intention of returning to Constantinople.

In a letter to Boccaccio dated at Venice, March 1, 1365 (*Sen.*, III, 6), Petrarch acquaints him with Leonzio's departure from Venice in the spring of 1364 (Koerting, *Petrarca*, p. 475), saying that he had presented the departing guest with a copy of Terence (in whose comedies Leonzio seemed to take such great delight) and had begged him to purchase for him in the East the works of Sophocles, Euripides, and of other classic Greek authors (*Sen.*, VI, 1). Petrarch adds that, prior to leaving, Leonzio had heaped vile abuse upon Italy and the Italians, but that he had no sooner touched the eastern shores of the Adriatic than, with characteristic fickleness, he had sent a long letter casting imprecations upon Greece and Constantinople. In *Seniles* V, 3 (of December 10, 1366, Koerting, *Bocc.*, p. 263, n. 2) Petrarch declares his firm resolve of never recalling Leonzio and of disregarding entirely all his prayers and entreaties. This letter shows bitter feeling against Leonzio, wherein Petrarch is goaded by the thought of the former's unfeeling and uncalled-for departure. The last letter pertaining to Leonzio's life (*Sen.*, VI, 1, of January 25 or 27, 1367, P. de Nolhac II, pp. 164, 165, and Koerting, *Bocc.*, p. 263, n. 2) is one full of compassion, for it gives an account of his death toward the end of 1366—how, during a storm at sea, Leonzio, like Ulysses, had strapped himself to the mast, and had been struck dead by a thunderbolt.

7. See above, n. 4.

8. Sen., *Contr.*, iii, *praef.*, 8: "Ciceronem eloquentia sua in carminibus destituit; Vergilium illa felicitas ingenii [sui] oratione soluta reliquit." Comparing with Frac., Vol. III, pp. 293, 294, it will be seen that Petrarch has adapted the above words to his construction.

9. For the poetical efforts of Cicero consult C. F. W. Mueller (Teubner, 1898), Vol. III, Pt. IV, pp. 350–405, "Fragmenta Poematum." As to Vergil, we gather that he must have written letters to Augustus from the words of Donatus (*Vita Verg.*, XII, 46, p. 61R). Macrobius (I, 24, 11) gives a five-line quotation from a letter of the poet to the emperor. In fact,

comparing the contents of this quotation with the statement in Donatus, it seems that the five lines are from the very letter referred to by the biographer.

10. St. Jerome, *Chron.*, II, *praef.* 2, end, in Migne, Vol. XXVII, coll. 223, 224. Petrarch quotes the same passage, and à propos of the same subject, in *Var.* 25. Consult n. 3 above, in which a lengthy extract from that letter is given. The present letter to Homer (*Fam.*, XXIV, 12) is dated October 9, 1360; *Var.* 25 to Boccaccio is dated August 18, 1360. If, then, the *aliquando* of the present letter alludes to *Var.* 25, it will be evident that the interval elapsed was but a short one.

11. The translation by Leonzio Pilato was made into Latin prose. The reference here, however, must be to the preliminary translation made at Padua in the winter of 1358–59 (cf. nn. 3 and 4). In *Var.* 25 Petrarch employs the same figure.

12. *Fam.*, XXIV, 10 (to Horace) and XXIV, 11 (to Vergil) are in the form of poetic epistles. In 1359 (cf. *Fam.*, XX, 7, note) Petrarch separated all those letters which he did not destroy into two groups: the prose epistles, which he dedicated to Socrates (*Fam.*, *praefatio*, I, pp.

15, 16, and *Fam.*, XXIV, 13), and the poetic epistles, which he dedicated to Barbato da Sulmona (*praef.*, *loc. cit.*, and *Fam.*, XXII, 3). The appearance in this collection, therefore, of the poetic epistles to Horace and to Vergil, must be due to their subject-matter, for they very naturally fall among those letters written "veteribus illustribus viris" (Vol. III, p. 306).

13. Apparently, Petrarch had received a letter purporting to be from the shade of Homer. The author of it is unknown. If it came from Florence, then of course it must have emanated from the circle of his Florentine friends. However, in Vol. 5, pp. 197, 198, Fracassetti, commenting upon the words, "Tua illa Bononia quam suspiras .... unum habet" (Vol. III, p. 301), but reading "qua suspiras," translates, "That Bologna of yours whence you send such laments," and hazards the suggestion that the letter to which this of Petrarch is a reply came from Bologna and not from Florence. We may go a step farther. Since Homeric scholars in Italy were so scarce at the time, and since Petrarch states that Bologna could boast of but one—Pietro di Muglio or de Muglo (cf. n. 31)—it would seem (if Fracassetti be right) that Pietro di Bologna was responsible for the

pseudo-Homer letter. As Messrs. Robinson and Rolfe perhaps justly remark of that letter (*Petrarch*, p. 253, n. 2): "It must have been even more interesting than this reply, in its unconscious revelation of mediaeval limitations."

14. In this instance Petrarch is carried away by his subject, and addresses his (to us unknown) correspondent as if he were the real Homer and a Greek. Compare what has been said on this subject in the preceding note.

15. The reference is to *Rem. utr. fort.*, I, 64, entitled *De aviariis avibusque loquacibus*—a most ridiculous place in which to find mention of the bard of Smyrna. On p. 193 one of the interlocutors says, "I own a most eloquent magpie." To which the other replies that it is absurd to apply such a term to a magpie, adding, "But if the magpie forthwith forget a word, either because the word is a difficult one or because of its own weak memory, it may even die of grief. Hence we must now consider less marvelous the death of the poet Homer, if indeed the current report be true"—"si tamen illa (mors) etiam vera est." The *De remediis* was begun in 1358 (Frac., I, p. 1, n. 1) and finished in 1366 (Torraca, I, Pt. II, p. 231).

Since the date of the Homer letter is October 9, 1360, it results that at least the first sixty-four chapters of Book I of the *De remediis* were written before this date. We see, too, that by this slight reference to Homer, Petrarch did give some currency to the report that Homer died of grief, and did add to it a note of uncertainty.

The story of Homer's death, as Petrarch and other mediaeval men knew it, must have been the one they found in Valerius Maximus; and though Petrarch does not actually cite him as his source, this clearly results from the references to Sophocles and to Philemon shortly following. Valerius, then, says (ix, 12, *ext.* 3):

> The cause of Homer's death too is said to have been an uncommon one. Having landed at the island of Ios, certain fishermen asked him a riddle which he was unable to read, in consequence of which Homer is believed to have died of grief.

The legend in its more complete form (unknown to Petrarch) is derived from the so-called *Lives* compiled from the minor poems falsely attributed to Homer. It runs as follows. On his way to Thebes, Homer landed at Ios, where he saw some young fishermen on the shore with their nets. In answer to his question as to what they had caught, the young fishermen propounded to him this riddle: "What we caught we left, what we caught not we bring." Homer was unable to read this riddle; and remembering an oracle which had foretold that he would die "through chagrin at his inability to read the riddle of the fishermen," he wrote an epitaph for himself and died of vexation and grief on the third day thereafter (cf. *New International Encycl.*, and the *Brit.*).

If Petrarch questioned the credibility of the shorter and simpler version of Valerius, what would he have said of this fuller legend, elaborated as it was with so many undignified frills?

16. Val. Max., ix, 12, *ext.* 5:

When Sophocles was already in extreme old age, he submitted one of his tragedies in competition at the games. For a long time he was very anxious concerning (as he thought) the doubtful decision of the judges. But his great joy when he was at last unanimously declared victor, brought about his death.

Cf. Pliny, *N. H.*, VII, 53, 180.

17. Fully to realize Petrarch's state of mind, it is necessary to quote substantial portions of his two sources for these statements. The first statement is again founded on Val. Max., ix, 12, *ext.* 6:

The strain of excessive laughter took off Philemon. Some figs had been prepared for him, but had been left in open view. Seeing a young ass eating them, Philemon summoned a boy to drive him away. The boy, however, answered the summons leisurely, arriving when all the figs had already been devoured. Whereupon Philemon said, "Since you have been so slow in coming, now give the ass some wine." And forthwith he began to roar at his own witty remark, panting hard until the irregular breathing in his aged throat choked him.

The second version, which Petrarch considers "more serious and more credible," is that of Apuleius, *Florida*, xvi:

For these praiseworthy qualities he (Philemon) was for a long time well known as a writer of comedies. It happened one day that he was giving a public reading of part of a play which he had recently written. When he had reached the third act .... a sudden rainstorm arose .... which compelled the gathering and the reading to be postponed. Upon being urgently pressed by several, Philemon promised that he would finish the reading on the very next day. And so on the following day a large throng of very eager men gathered in the theater. .... But when they had sat waiting longer than seemed reasonable, and when Philemon did not put in an appearance, several of the more eager were sent to summon him, and found him dead in his bed. .... Returning thence they reported to the expectant audience that the poet Philemon, whom they were so eagerly attending, to hear him complete the reading of his latest play, had already, and at his own home, brought a real drama to a close.

In his manuscript of the *Florida*, Petrarch wrote the following marginal note to this passage: "This version of the death of Philemon is somewhat nobler than the one related by Valerius and, indeed, by myself; for in a certain letter of mine I followed both him and the current opinion." P. de Nolhac says that he has not been able to find the letter referred to by Petrarch (II, p. 102, and n. 4). The present epistle to Homer was written in 1360; and it may well be that the letter referred to was destroyed in the general holocaust of 1359, when Petrarch sorted his correspondence into the two collections (cf. above, n. 12). Moreover, it was just like the careful Petrarch to destroy a wrong version when he had once learned the true one.

18. On the general similarity between the *Odyssey* and the *Aeneid*, Petrarch says (*Rer. mem.*, III, 3, "De sapienter dictis vel factis," p. 456):

Homer describes his Ulysses (in whom he means to give the type of a wise and brave man) as wandering over lands and seas, and in his poem makes him encircle nearly the entire world. Our poet has followed this example; he too carries his Aeneas over the different countries of the earth. Both poets have done so designedly; for wisdom can hardly be gained without experience nor can experience be had by one who does not see and observe many things. And, finally, it is hard to understand how one can see many things if he stirs not abroad, but sticks close to one little corner of this earth.

Petrarch enters upon a more general discussion of the two poets, quoting from Macrobius and others, in *Rer. mem.*, II, 2, "De ingenio," p. 413:

Among the Greeks Homer reigns supreme in the intellectual world. Of this dictum not I, but Pliny is the author, who ascribes to him a richer, broader, and boundless glory [cf. Pliny, *N. H.*, ii, 6; xxv, 2 (5)]. It is perfectly clear that with the aid of his divine genius Homer has solved a large number of philosophical problems in a far better and more decisive fashion than the professed philosophers themselves. Macrobius with great assurance pronounces Homer the fountain-head and source of all divine inspiration [Comm. in Somn. Scip., ii, 10, 11]. And rightly so. For although tradition has it that Homer was physically blind, his soul was so clear and luminous that Tullius says of him in the Tusculans [v, 114]: "His verses are as a painting, not poetry. What country, what coast, what part of Greece, what manner of battle and array of soldiers, what army, what fleet, what motions of men and of beasts have not been depicted by him with such skill as to make it possible for us to see what he himself did not see?" But why should I discourse on his eloquence, since in the oft-cited books of the *Saturnalia* there is drawn an extensive and undecided parallel between our poet and the Greek [book v entire]? In the course of a thousand and one arguments, now this one is proved superior, now that one, and shortly they are shown to be equal [*Sat.*, v, 12, 1]. In consequence these arguments leave the reader doubtful of the issue—an uncertainty admirably expressed by the satirist in these verses [Juvenal, xi, 180, 181, ed. Fried., translated by Gifford, II, p. 161]:

"Great Homer shall his deep-ton'd thunder roll,
And mighty Maro elevate the soul;
Maro, who, warm'd with all the poet's fire,
Disputes the palm of victory with his sire."

19. Horace, *Sat.*, i, 5, 41, 42.

20. Macrobius gives us an example of the accusation generally made in antiquity against Vergil—*Sat.*, v, 3, 16:

Continue prithee, said Avienus, to trace all that he [Vergil] borrowed from Homer. For what can be sweeter than to hear two pre-eminent poets voicing the same thoughts? These three things are held to be equally impossible: to steal either the lightning of Jove, or the club of Hercules, or the verses of Homer, and for the reason that, even if it were possible, it would seem unbecoming for any other than Jove to hurl the lightning, any other than Hercules to excel in physical strength, any other than Homer to sing the verses he sang. Still, this author [Vergil] has opportunely embodied in his poem that which the earlier bard had sung, making it appear that it is his own.

The retort referred to is not to be found in the *Saturnalia* (a slip on Petrarch's part), but in St. Jerome, who says (*Praefatio lib. hebr. quaest. in Genesim*, Migne, Vol. XXIII, col. 983):

Also the bard of Mantua was criticised by his rivals in this way [*sc.*, as Terence by Luscius Lanuvinus]. For, having used, unchanged, certain verses of Homer, he was called a mere compiler of the earlier poets. To which he replied that it was a sign of great power to wrest the club from the hands of Hercules—"magnarum esse virium clavam Herculi extorquere de manu."

With this compare Frac., III, p. 298. St. Jerome himself, however, must have been quoting from the life by Donatus, and in so doing gave a different turn to the reply. Donatus says (*Vita Verg.*, XVI, 64, p. 66R) that Vergil replied: "Why did not they too attempt the same thefts? They would discover that it is easier to steal the club of Hercules than to pilfer a verse from Homer."

Petrarch's purpose is to emphasize how vigorous a poet Vergil is, and how worthy of following in Homer's footsteps. Hence he does not have recourse to the more ancient defense which was ready to his hand in Macrobius, *Sat.*, VI, 3, 1, to the effect that it was the earlier Roman poets who stole from Homer, and that Vergil borrowed from these earlier pilferers belonging to his own race. Such line of argument would have made Vergil the second thief, but it would not have made his verses the best stolen.

21. Lucan, *Pharsalia*, ix, 980–86 (tr. by Edw. Ridley, p. 299, vss. 1157–66):

> O sacred task of poets, toil supreme,
> Which rescuing all things from allotted fate
> Dost give eternity to mortal men!
> Grudge not the glory, Caesar, of such fame.
> For if the Latian Muse may promise aught,
> Long as the heroes of the Trojan time
> Shall live upon the page of Smyrna's bard,
> So long shall future races read of thee
> In this my poem; and Pharsalia's song
> Live unforgotten in the age to come.

22. Horace, *Ars Poetica*, 396–401, and *Carm.*, iv. 9, vss. 5, 6.

23. Theocritus in *Ecl.*, iv, 1, and vi, 1; Hesiod in *Georg.*, ii, 176.

24. Statius, *Theb.*, xii, 816, 817.

25. In Petrarch's days the *Appendix Vergiliana* was known as the *Ludi Iuveniles*, and included what is now published by Baehrens

in the *Poetae latini minores*, Vol. II. Judging from the statement of the present letter, Petrarch was acquainted with these *Ludi*, or with some of them at least. Boccaccio was the first to add the eighty *Priapea* to his codex of the *Ludi* (Sabbadini, p. 32). Sabbadini, p. 24 and n. 5, gives proof that Petrarch knew the *Culex* and the *Rosae*, and on p. 31 adds that he was furthermore acquainted with some of the *Catalecta*, without giving proof.

In this letter to Homer, Petrarch states that the former's name is mentioned in the *Ludi*. The total number of references to Homer in the *Appendix Vergiliana* is four: *Ciris*, 65; in the epigram closing the *Catalecta*, vs. 2; *Priapea*, 68, 4, and 80, 5. In the *Rendiconti del R. Ist. Lomb.* (1906, p. 386), Sabbadini remarks at this point: "A quali e a quanti dei tre componimenti alludesse il Petrarca, non ci é dato indovinare, ma ciascuno dei tre era a quei tempi una cospicua novitá." Personally we should be inclined to favor the *Ciris* and the *Catalecta*, and, indeed, to give the latter reference in support of the statement of Sabbadini on p. 31. But until further proof is found, all discussion on this point is merely idle speculation.

26. Donatus, in speaking of Vergil, says (p. 65R): "Vergil never lacked detractors; and no wonder: even Homer had his."

27. This, of course, is a reference to some statement occurring in the pseudo-Homer letter which Petrarch had received.

28. See above, n. 22.

29. Petrarch's words are: "cum verissime dicat hebraeus Sapiens quod '*stultorum infinitus est numerus*'" (III, p. 301). From the manner of Petrarch's quoting, and from the fact that Fracassetti italicizes the words in single quotation marks, it would be inferred that the citation is from the Bible. But an exhaustive search through the Concordances of both Cruden and Young has failed to reveal such a passage, though sentiments on the subject of folly and fools are quite numerous. It may be, of course, that Petrarch epitomized, or rather formulated a deduction of his own from the books of Proverbs and Ecclesiastes.

30. Concerning the nationality of Leonzio Pilato consult what has been said above in n. 3, par. 1.

31. It is generally agreed that of the three scholars said to be at Florence, Boccaccio must be one. The other two cannot be identified

with certainty, but they are to be chosen from among Nelli, Salutati, and Bruni; of no one of whom, however, do we know as a fact that he was acquainted with Greek. It is for this reason that Tedaldo della Casa, who studied Greek under Leonzio Pilato, has, with greater probability, been suggested as one of the three Florentines (Baldelli). Petrarch himself has been thought of by De Sade as the fourth, but (it seems) on insufficient grounds. The fifth Florentine is without doubt Zanobi de Strada, who in 1359 was appointed apostolic secretary by Innocent VI, and who in consequence abandoned Naples and Italy for Avignon, the Babylon across the Alps.

The scholar at Bologna, too, can be named: Pietro di Muglio or de Muglo (cf. n. 13). The Veronese humanists are Guglielmo da Pastrengo and Rinaldo da Villafranca. The Mantuan, according to De Sade and Tiraboschi, is Andrea (surnamed) Mantovano; and the one from Perugia, finally, has been variously identified with Paolo Perugino (Baldelli) and Muzio da Perugia (De Sade and Tiraboschi). Fracassetti (Vol. 5, p. 197) has omitted all mention of the humanist at Sulmona, who very probably is to be identified with Marco Barbato da Sulmona. (Consult Frac., *loc. cit.*, who gives some cross-references to his own notes; and Voigt.)

32. Cf. n. 1.

33. This note of despair was wrung from Petrarch by his dismay at the existent state of affairs and by his own high ideals of scholarship. That it eventually proved to be an utterly false prophecy was due mainly to the vigorous impulse which he himself gave to the cause of humanism.

34. Cf. n. 15.

35. The famous words from the epitaph of Ennius (Cic., *Tusc.*, i, 34), which Petrarch has here adapted to his purpose by the insertion of the bracketed words, "(Nam) volito vivus (docta) per ora virum" (Frac., III, p. 303).

36. Petrarch had owned a Greek Homer as early as 1354, when his friend Niccoló Sigero sent him a copy from Constantinople (cf. n. 3, par. 2). *Fam.*, XVIII, 2, describes Petrarch's joy at its reception, and also his sorrow at not being able to understand a word of it, which clearly proves that the first modern scholar had not made much progress after a summer's instruction from the first teacher of Greek in the western world (see n. 1). In Latin, Petrarch had the *Periochae* which are attributed to

Ausonius and the *Homerus Latinus* or *Pindarus Thebanus* (for which see n. 5).

37. Fond hopes was Petrarch nourishing, and vain! We must remember that when Leonzio Pilato finished his translation of Homer in 1363, there was but one copy of it, and that that copy remained at Florence. We can well imagine Petrarch's eagerness to peruse it. His first inquiry is made in *Seniles*, III, 6 (of March 1, 1365), by which letter he requests that some portion at least of the *Odyssey* be forwarded to him, continuing that he is quite content to wait for the rest. From *Seniles* V, 1 (Padua, December 14, 1365, Koerting, *Bocc.*, p. 263, n. 2), we learn that when Boccaccio received this pressing note, the *Iliad* had already been transcribed; and so he hastened to make with his own hand a transcription of that passage in the *Odyssey* describing the descent of Ulysses to Hades. In the same letter Petrarch expresses satisfaction at hearing that this is at last on its way to him. Through some mishap, however, the precious package had not yet reached its destination at Venice by the 25th or 27th of January, 1367 (*Sen.*, VI, 1; Koerting, *op. cit.*; P. de Nolhac, II, p. 165). The joy of Petrarch, when he at last grasped the translation of Homer

with his own hands and beheld it among the books on his own shelves, is simply expressed in the closing words of *Seniles* VI, 2 (undated, but later than VI, 1). To conclude, the translation, which was begun by Leonzio in the latter half of 1360 (the date of *Fam.*, XXIV, 12), did not reach him who was the most eager for it till seven years later.

A SELECTED BIBLIOGRAPHY

BAEUMKER, KLEMENS. *Quibus antiquis auctoribus Petrarca in conscribendis rerum memorabilium libris usus sit.* Muenster, 1882.

BURCKHARDT, JACOB. *The Civilisation of the Renaissance in Italy.* Translated by S. G. C. Middlemore. London: Swan Sonnenschein & Co., 1898.

BUTLER, H. E. *Sexti Properti opera omnia.* With a commentary. London: Archibald Constable & Co., 1905.

COMPARETTI, DOMENICO. *Vergil in the Middle Ages.* Translated by E. F. M. Benecke. London; Swan Sonnenschein & Co., 1895.

CONINGTON, JOHN. *The Aeneid of Virgil. Translated into English Verse.* 10th ed. Longmans, Green and Co., 1900.

DASSAMINIATO, GIOVANNI. *De' rimedii dell' una e dell' altra fortuna, volgarizzati nel buon secolo della lingua.* Published by Casimiro Stolfi at Bologna, presso Gaetano Romagnoli, 1867. 2 vols. (In *Collezione di opere inedite o rare dei primi tre secoli della lingua*, Vols. XVII and XVIII.)

DEVELAY, VICTOR. A translation of the letters to Cicero, in *Bulletin du bibliophile et du bibliothécaire* (1881), pp. 213-19; of the letter to Seneca, *ibid.*, pp. 289-95; to Varro, *ibid.*, pp. 385-88; to Quintilian, Livy, Pollio, and Horace, *ibid.*, pp. 481-93.

FRACASSETTI, GIUSEPPE. *Francisci Petrarcae epistolae de rebus familiaribus et variae . . . . studio et cura Iosephi Fracassetti. Florentiae, typis Felicis Le Monnier.* 3 vols., 1859–63.

———. *Lettere di Francesco Petrarca delle cose familiari libri ventiquattro, lettere varie libro unico. Volgarizzate e dichiarate con note da G. F.* Firenze, Successori Le Monnier, 1892. 5 vols.

———. *Lettere senili di Francesco Petrarca. Volgarizzate e dichiarate con note da G. F.* Firenze, Successori Le Monnier, 1892, 2 vols. (In *Biblioteca Nazionale Economica*.)

GIBBON, EDWARD. *The History of the Decline and Fall of the Roman Empire.* Edited by J. B. Bury. London: Methuen & Co., 1900. 7 vols.

GIFFORD, Wm. *The Satires of D. J. Juvenal*, Philadelphia, 1803.

GREGOROVIUS, FERDINAND. *History of the City of Rome in the Middle Ages.* Translated by Annie Hamilton. London: George Bell & Sons.

HALLAM, HENRY. *View of the State of Europe during the Middle Ages.* 9th ed. London: John Murray, 1846.

HARRIS, ELLA ISABEL. *The Tragedies of Seneca.* Oxford, 1904.

KOERTING, GUSTAV. *Geschichte der Litteratur Italiens im Zeitalter der Renaissance.* Vol. I, "Petrarca's Leben und Werke," Leipzig, 1878; Vol. II, "Boccaccio's Leben und Werke," Leipzig, 1880.

LODGE, R. *The Close of the Middle Ages, 1273–1494.* London: Rivingtons, 1902.

MIGNE, J. P. *Patrologiae cursus completus.* Paris.

MOORE, CH. R. *The Elegies of Propertius.* London: Rivingtons, 1870.

NETTLESHIP, H. *Ancient Lives of Vergil.* Oxford, 1879.

——. *Vergil.* In "Classical Writers." New York, D. Appleton & Co., 1880.

NOLHAC, PIERRE DE. *Pétrarque et l'humanisme.* In *Bibliothèque littéraire de la renaissance, Nouvelle Série.* 2 vols. Paris: Honoré Champion, 1907.

PETRARCH, F. *Opera quae extant omnia .... haec quidem omnia nunc iterum .... repurgata .... et in tomos quator distincta .... Basileae, per Sebastianum Henricpetri.* 1581, folio, 4 vols. in one, and paged continuously.

——. *De Remediis utriusque fortunae libri duo, eiusdem De contemptu mundi colloquiorum liber quem secretum suum inscripsit. Roterodami, ex officina Arnoldi Leers,* 1649.

REIFFERSCHEID, AUGUSTUS. *C. Suetoni Tranquilli reliquiae.* Lipsiae: Teubner, 1860.

RIDLEY, EDW. *The Pharsalia of Lucan, Translated into Blank Verse.* Longmans, Green & Co., 1896.

ROBINSON, JAS. H., AND ROLFE, HENRY W. *Petrarch, the First Modern Scholar and Man of Letters.* Putnam's Sons, 1898.

SABBADINI, REMIGIO. *Le Scoperte dei codici latini e greci ne' secoli XIV e XV.* Firenze: G. C. Sansoni, 1905.

——. "Il primo nucleo della biblioteca del Petrarca," *Rendiconti del R. istituto lombardo* (1906), pp. 369-88.

——. "Quali biografie vergiliane fossero note al Petrarca," *ibid.*, pp. 193-98.

SABBADINI, REMIGIO. "La Vergilii vita di Donato," *Studi italiani di filologia classica*, Vol. V, pp. 384–88.

SERVII *Grammatici qui feruntur in Vergilii carmina commentarii. Recensuerunt* GEORGIUS THILO *et* HERMANNUS HAGEN. 3 vols. Teubner.

SYMONDS, JOHN ADDINGTON. *Renaissance in Italy*.

———. The article on "Petrarch" in the *Encycl. Brit.* (new Werner ed.).

VOIGT, GEORG. *Die Wiederbelebung des classischen Alterthums, oder das erste Jahrhundert des Humanismus.* 2 vols., 3d ed., by Georg Reimer, Berlin, 1893.

———. "Die Briefsammlungen Petrarcas und der venetianische Staatskanzler Benintendi, *Abh. d. III. Cl. d. k. Ak. d. Wiss.*, XVI Bd., III. Abth., pp. 1–101. Muenchen, 1883.

CPSIA information can be obtained at www.ICGtesting.com
Printed in the USA
BVOW07s2048130314

347610BV00005B/69/P